Contents

Introduction

Cars = sex. That was the logic. As a teenager growing up in rural Leicestershire, in a time before mobile phones, Internet and other ways to communicate with the fairer sex, having a car was essential. The feeling of freedom, having your own house on wheels with tunes, reclining seats and somewhere private to take Tracey from checkout 6 for an evening's fumble is one that will be familiar to many readers. I suspect that, with the benefit of hindsight, statistically quite a few readers also probably had the pleasure of Tracey from checkout 6. Anyway, you'll be familiar with the thrill of being able to escape on a whim and enjoy the open road, even in something as primitive as a Vauxhall Chevette, which was my first car. I wasn't really into cars as a kid. They were a means to an end and, even now, I tend to glaze over when chaps enthuse about the 0–60 mph time of their latest hot hatch. What has always stuck with me is the desire to explore.

Like many readers though, I always found it nigh on impossible to escape my responsibilities for weeks on end to drive to Timbuktu, as appealing as it sounds. There seems to be no shortage of banger rallies, almost exclusively all with a name ending in 'ball' or 'run', culminating with unwanted knowledge of how long it takes a recovery truck to find you at the side of a rainswept Belgian motorway. Belgium is also part of the problem with that kind of trip. Escaping the traffic hell of the UK is bad enough, but reaching much of the best bits of Europe for driving seems to involve having to traverse Belgium on pot-holed, congested motorways. In short; your banger rally will probably take 24 hours to get you to the start of anything remotely interesting. And a convoy of cars will attract attention. There are cases of banger rallyists crashing after falling asleep at the wheel or otherwise antagonising German Polizei who won't find a VW Sharan decorated as a tank amusing in any way. I'm too old and grumpy to put up with foreign rozzers if at all avoidable.

And then there's the cost of an organised rally; buying, prepping, taxing and insuring a banger is more costly than you might first estimate. And finding someone to provide breakdown cover might be a challenge. And, when the fun is over, you either have to drive the thing home (via broken Belgium again), where you'll find that your shagged out car is unwanted on eBay, or you have to abandon it abroad and stress about being tracked down by some persistent foreign authority who took a dislike to you leaving your car behind. Yes, these charity rallies often raise lots for charity, but I find doing my own thing cheaper, less hassle and more fun. And that's what it's about: fun. A combination of budget airlines, car hire (always ticking the 'insurance excess waiver' box) and charging around foreign mountains is, in my experience, quicker, cheaper and considerably more fun than risking your own metal. It was PJ O'Rourke who said "nothing handles like a rental" and I wholeheartedly agree. I have had more fun in rented Korean hatchbacks on the Continent than I have sat in supercars in London traffic.

There needs to be a reason for a road trip. Driving to Spain or wherever because you've come up with a natty name isn't enough. When trying to cajole a mate into joining me on 'Omega to Riga', he cowardly countered with 'Fiesta to Leicester'. A pun alone is not sufficient reason to buy an ex-Caravan Club Vauxhall and drive across Europe to end up in Latvia where, almost unfailingly, Brits looking for a bit of weekend debauchery at the end of a long drive seem to end up getting mugged. And then they must drive home. Via Belgium. There are a few popular trips that never really excited me. Land's End to John O' Groats (also known as LeJoG) looks, for example, like two miserable places joined by lots of camera-controlled motorway. Living in the Midlands means that I would effectively have to do the trip twice anyway: once to get down to the start, drive past my house in the middle bit on the way up north and then back down to my house at the end. That's a lot of motorway.

There are some trips that I wish I had thought of. You might recall a man called Craig Williams who decided to drive a Vauxhall Frontera up the little railway track that runs up Mount Snowdon in Wales. Almost worth the 22-month prison sentence he was slapped with for the adventure. There are some grand trips abroad, such as the Mongol Rally, but these take more time, money and diplomacy with bent foreign officials than I could ever muster. For me, the winning formula is 2–3 days abroad, a budget airline flight, a boggo rental car (less is more) and some utterly lethal switchbacks somewhere in the sun, retracing the route of some historic tally-ho heroics.

I like to visit forgotten racetracks for example. A lot of early motorsport was conducted on public roads. Roads that still exist. Rally stages, highest roads and other unusual geographical landmarks also make for great destinations. I am deeply indebted to Google Maps. Many an hour has been spent happily 'driving' distant hairpins on Google Street View. Some are easily accessed, others require a bit of guile and a few (no one is reading this, right?) demand wrangling skills of the highest order—or outright trespass. I've always been better at wrangling than driving. As my addiction to exploring took hold, I started to find other interesting destinations, sometimes completely by chance (see "Joop's Greenhouse", later in this book), usually in something with a rental sticker in the windscreen. That said, perhaps the funniest stunt ever was done on foot, in army surplus shoes. It was a drunken lap of Goodwood, which, when published, got me blacklisted, but once I have an idea, I find it hard to stop it from actually happening. If you want to do something enough, you'll find a way of making it happen.

There may well be rental company management reading this and getting a bit narky at my behaviour. There's also probably rental company employees thinking "that's nothing, we barrel rolled a Renault Espace in the short stay at Gatwick airport once". The aim of my automotive adventures is not to *deliberately* cause damage to the cars. I've always reported any damage caused, as I wouldn't want to leave a car in an unfit state for some unsuspecting family to rent. When paying the insurance excess waiver (essential, in my experience), there is usually no financial penalty for any damage caused, so there's no incentive to hide anything. Considering that these trips were typically only a few days long, the cost of the excess, in the grand scheme of things, is negligible.

In a peculiar twist, my mucking about abroad led to me becoming a writer for car mags, then a presenter on YouTube and then some (obscure and mostly unwatched) telly work. This book is a bit of a 'how to' cookbook for those seeking a quick fix of low-cost motoring fun abroad and, also, the story of how that led onto other jollies— even, eventually, making a few bob from it. From that first low-cost jolly, I ended up getting paid to drive a supercar on a closed racetrack in France and talk bollocks to a camera. Not even the fusty delights of Tracey from checkout 6 could beat this. *Nothing* handles like a rental.

Stelvio

Car;   Rented Fiat 500 1.2. Looks and rides like a
                rubber dog chew.

Location;   From Orio del Serio airport, Bergamo, to
                the Stelvio Pass, Italy.

Duration;   24 hours plus flights there and back.

P. J. O'Rourke coined the phrase "nothing handles like a
rental car". I wasn't setting out to emulate him but to
instead enjoy a weekend thrash up one of the most iconic
Alpine passes in Europe, at a sensible price. It would
mean hiring something cheap and cheerful. Well, we paid
for cheap, any cheerful would be a bonus. This was one of
the first trips I did and it set the standard for many
subsequent automotive adventures.

A £50 flight from what Ryanair calls London to what Ryanair calls Milan, £3 for what Ryanair calls coffee and £60 for 24 hours in a hire car with all the insurance boxes ticked gets you to the Stelvio Pass. Play your cars [sic] right and the rental company will give you a cheerful Fiat 500 instead of the usual fodder. After a last-minute row with the missus, and playing my trump card "Waste of money? You own 150 pairs of shoes!", there I was, zipping along an Autostrada with co-pilot Dr. Darryl Octane and five identical cars driven by mates in close formation. Grinning. Massively.

Bormio is a town approximately 2 hours drive north of what Ryanair calls Milan and sits at the foot of the Stelvio Pass. The pass itself is well signposted and the road started promisingly: two lanes, decent tarmac and no traffic as we approached from the south, the only traffic being the odd battered Piaggio Ape. Signs warn of 'tornati' (meaning hairpins), you crick your neck looking up/round the turns, 2nd gear corners become 1st gear corners, 4th and 5th gears become completely redundant and you climb higher. The road begins to narrow, rusty Armco on one side, mountain on the other, through dingy tunnels, making good use of the lights and horn. The CD player had the obligatory Matt Monroe disc playing but, in true Italian fashion, it stopped working for no reason. The last section climbing Stelvio from the south is stunning: short straights, 180-degree corners and breathtaking views. The temperature drops and curves become consecutive switchbacks, the Fiat screaming like an Italian footballer after being kicked in the knackers. Maybe we were lucky, but we didn't get stuck behind anyone/thing, the sun shone and we had this heavenly bit of mountain to ourselves for the afternoon.

The hairpins eventually straighten out across a plateau at the top, we stretched the Fiat up through the gears until happening upon a cow in the road, braking late to overtake a local (1.2 Fiat trumping 4.0 Jeep), before finally pulling into a little car park at the top. The view is simply stunning from up there and the air clear and crisp.

After an impromptu snowball fight and a wurst, we started the descent, heading north. This was bloody hard work, the little Fiat's brakes overheating after a mile or two. Snow thrown at the calipers helped cool things. We had to stand upwind of the stench. Clutch, brakes and boiled snow polluting the previously pristine Alpine air.

We turned round and headed back over the top and down the south face back towards Bormio. The smoking brakes completely gave up halfway down, so we grabbed some pictures against one of the countless stunning backdrops. The CD player decided to start working again.

The beauty of the surrounding snow-capped mountains cannot be adequately captured on camera, but we went for the driving, not just the sightseeing. There are those who claim Stelvio isn't much fun. These people are to be ignored. Admittedly, we had perfect weather and no traffic. The cars were designed for mincing down to the shops, not being tortured up an alp, but this is about expectations. You expect such a car driven here to be horrible, hateful, even. But it's not. You learn to work around its shortcomings, even though no power and no brakes didn't leave much to work with. And then you bond with it, before throwing it into another 180-degree turn and making it lean like a 2CV because the speed you've built up is too precious to be wasted by braking.

The previous night on the way there, we'd taken a diversion over the Foppa Pass (confusingly, also called the Mortirolo Pass), which is heavily wooded, occasionally gravelly and huge fun. I learned all my Latin from Life of

Brian and can, therefore, only manage "People called Romanes they go the house", but Mortirolo made me think of 'mort', which I think means death. I had seen some monuments online to expired cyclists here and thought I'd have a stab from the relative safety of a hire car.

On the way back, we planned to take another diversion via the lesser-known Gavia Pass, which starts a short drive away from Bormio. The way up was easy enough: some typically tight hairpins through the trees bringing you out on a wide barren plateau above the treeline, with a glacier as the backdrop. We stopped again at an Italian war memorial to take in the views and let the Fiats catch their breath.

It is difficult to find the words to describe the next stage; the words on the in-car video are almost exclusively expletives, the Bond theme "You Only Live Twice" playing in the background... As we bounced at speed across the top of the plateau in the 500s, we came to the top of the descent, the first hairpin had the usual rusty Armco, but the straights generally had only the odd kerbstone. As passenger for this leg (I had done the drive up), I was looking at a few inches of fractured tarmac and a drop down into the misty clouds below. There was a strange silence, like the clouds below us had soaked up the sound. The road down is just 1.5 cars wide and had some longish straights, making it too easy to build up decentish speed and forget the brakes are knackered. The exits of corners are often missing kerbstones, leaving a nice Fiat-sized gap with cold mountain air as your run-off. How we squeezed past a German campervan crawling up the road without putting two wheels over the edge I'll never know. I could smell their fear as we screamed past. There would have been time to write my will during the tumble off the side of the mountain before hitting the bottom of the valley below. By now, we all knew the limitations of our cars. We were feeling fatigue, fear and the indescribable thrill of ripping along a road better described as a ledge cut into a rock face.

Our first casualty was almost inevitable. Nose first, off
went the car into a small ravine, brakes having totally
given up finally. The call to the rental company was
creative. "It has broken down". The driver (who shall
remain nameless) scrounged a lift to the nearest branch
of the rental company and we didn't see him again for
hours. We ended up in a lovely little hotel, drank grappa,
ate pizza and laughed with relief at having gotten away
with it. Then came a phone call. Only one of us was sober
enough to drive, so we all packed into a Fiat 500 like a
proper 1950s Catholic family holiday to meet the mate
who had gotten a replacement car and wanted to meet us
at the crash site. The weight was too much for the Fiat on
the steeper slopes, so we took it in turns to walk
alongside the 500. On arriving at the ravine, in the
freezing dark, it became clear that we had more trouble.

The rental company had replaced the 'broken down' car
with an Opel Agila and told the driver that a recovery

truck would fetch the 'broken down' car in the morning. Fearing trouble for having left the car in a ravine, he wanted to move it (on his own) into a more respectable position and blame the damage on bears or something. His tow rope, procured from God knows where, was too short and meant that the Opel had to drive nose first to the very edge of the precipice in order for the rope to reach the Fiat. Best boy scout knot applied, he had jumped in the Opel and somehow moved forwards the couple of millimetres required for it to end up dangling as well! At that point, he had called us.

Drunk and laughing, we pushed it back onto the road and someone found another rope, lashed it to the first rope and we attempted to pull the Fiat back onto the tarmac. The Opel's engine screamed like a tortured animal, the clutch slipped and it stank. We all pushed. The Fiat was done for. It never moved an inch in the ravine. Now we had an Opel with no clutch and a horrendous electrical smell inside the cabin complete with disco lights on the dash. We had to abandon both cars and now the rental company would know exactly what we'd been up to. The tow rope was so taut we couldn't undo the knot, and no one had a knife. But someone did have a fag lighter... We sat in/on the remaining 500 and coasted downhill for miles with the suspension bottoming out and, as we reached the bottom of the mountain, we saw blue lights flashing half a mile or so above us. Fire brigade, perhaps?

The following morning, we started the drive back to the airport. We had two punctures caused by sodding great lumps of rock that had rolled onto the road. The Fiat drank only €40 of unleaded during the trip and (despite crap on-the-limit brakes) was the perfect steer for the drive. No, really. The super-tight hairpins, sharp elevations, narrow roads and cruddy surface would have ruined most things this side of a Land Rover. Saying 'Cinquecento' might mark you out as a bit of a prat at home but, as the saying nearly goes, 'when in Milano'… We dropped the 500s' keys back at the rental desk 5 minutes before our 24-hour rental period ended, shrugging at the battle scars and scorched tyres and pointing at the ticked 'super extra insurance cover' box before squeezing ourselves aboard the Ryanair flight home. O'Rourke might have coined the phrase "nothing handles like a rental car", but we had made it our own.

A friend of a friend suggested that a magazine might be interested in my story (albeit without the incriminating bits), so I sent it to Practical Performance Car magazine, who straightened out my atrocious grammar and ran it as a front-cover feature. I soon became a features writer for them and they egged me on to attempt other trips, and gave me a bit of pocket money to help fund things.

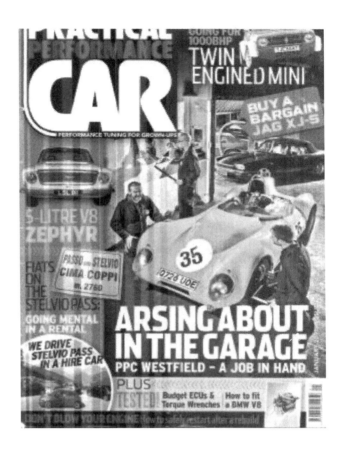

Re-tracing Paddy Hopkirk's 1964 Monte Carlo Rally win

Car;   Rented MINI Cooper cabriolet automatic.
                A name that loses appeal with each word
                uttered.

Location;   Nice, Col de Turini, France, then Monaco.

Duration;   24 hours plus flights there and back.

An easyJet flight from Luton, declining the microwaved mess of an in-flight meal, and Dr. O and I landed at Côte d'Azur airport in the south of France. Presenting our papers at the rental desk, we collected the keys to our car. I was driving as Dr. O's licence had been repeatedly tainted by the dark hand of the DVLA. The car was a MINI. No, the caps lock isn't stuck on this keyboard and I am not shouting. Since BMW's re-working of Rover's remnants, the ancient but beloved Mini has had a considerable makeover, as you may have noticed, and is now branded as (brace yourself) MINI. Hertz (other rental companies are available, dearest reader) had a deal where you could pick a specific car as part of their 'fun' range. Essentially, you paid a premium *not* to be given a diesel Peugeot or a 1.1 litre Chevrolet Frenulum. For this trip, only a MINI would do.

Our plan was to re-trace the route of the 1964 Monte Carlo Rally and, more specifically, the exploits of perhaps one of the UK's greatest motorsport underdogs—Paddy Hopkirk. Hopkirk started in Belfast with an archaic Harding 22 donated to him by a local priest, moving on to win the Rally of Ireland and then, following some success in the UK, he found himself driving a Mini for British Motor Company (BMC) in the 1964 Monte Carlo Rally.

In '64, the Rally was essentially a long-distance endurance rally with various starting points covering half of continental Europe, with some fast, timed stages on largely unsuitable roads towards the finish line in Monaco. Hopkirk chose to start in Minsk, then in Russia, because he hadn't been behind the iron curtain before. We started in Luton, then in Bedfordshire, because easyJet flew from there. The focus of our driving was on the final stages, starting with the infamous 'Col de Turini' stage, known as the 'Night of the Long Knives', as pale headlamps struggled to penetrate the January darkness a mile high in the mountains of the Mercantour National Park. Having already driven nearly 3000 miles on the rally (many of the entrants having already fallen by the wayside), Hopkirk got stuck into the stage between the mountain villages of La Bollène-Vésubie and Sospel. Dr. O, having discovered and demolished my emergency hip flask of rum, gave vague and increasingly aggressive directions as to what was the start point and we picked up the route from there in our MINI.

Hopkirk's Mini Cooper and our MINI Cooper share an undeniable design ethos. With modest power from an uncomplicated four cylinder normally aspirated engine, both cars depend on grip, balance and agility to make swift progress. Hopkirk's main rivals included the Ford Falcon piloted by Swede Bosse Ljungberg, a 5.7 litre V8-engined monster with three times the power of the little Mini. Fellow Swede Erik 'On the Roof' Karlsson drove a free-wheeling Saab 96. He earned his sobriquet with a penchant for exiting rallies upside down. Tom 'Horseman of the Apocalypse' Trana was another gloriously named Scandinavian, piloting a hunchbacked Volvo 544. All three Citroën DS19 works cars retired with various mechanical failures.

My main challenge seemed to be the sobriety of my co-driver. In '64, Hopkirk had filled his washer bottle with gin to prevent it from freezing and I had brought along a bottle of Tanqueray in the spirit of the original event. Yet, my navigator had succumbed to a terrible thirst and whilst I was preoccupied with yet another slippery 180-degree 1-in-4 hairpin, he had downed my booze before I could use it. As I martyred my tyres, he became agitated by the lack of *amuse-bouche* on board and could not be placated with the 'mood lighting' function on our modern MINI nor the shocking racket that passes for French radio. Hopkirk would not have approved, but he suffered from similar distractions. His car was stopped by the local gendarmerie who breathalysed his co-driver, Henry Liddon, before realising that the Mini Cooper was actually right-hand drive. He was also apprehended for driving the wrong way down a one-way street, fobbing off the officer with a tale about attending a funeral, yet his pace was relentless.

Capable of braking later and harder than bigger cars, Hopkirk edged into a slender lead in the snow. Although the Scandinavians had tremendous experience in the wintery conditions, they too were being hounded by the Mercedes 300 of Eugen Böhringer, a German ex-P.O.W. of the British, who had abandoned his restaurant business in Stuttgart for rallying to settle a bet with a friend. The Col de Turini's highest point (5282 feet) is now marked by a rather agreeable café, and whilst they didn't serve tea as you or I would recognise, their earthy coffee was a welcome pick-me-up for both me and my befuddled co-driver. On the descent, realising that he had, so far, been nothing more than ballast, he decided to help by giving instructions—"hairpin left, 200 over crest, 50, tightens, hairpin right, 50", which got on my tits after all of half a mile; "STOP TALKING TO ME, I'M TRYING TO BLOODY DRIVE!" We walloped down the mountain to Monaco, where the final stage took place.

Hopkirk was paid £40 a day in '64, a wage he was happy with, but today that scarcely covers petit fours in Monaco. We stayed at the Columbus Hotel, once owned by Formula 1 driver David Coulthard. The hotel is decorated in an avant-garde style but has an excellent bar and lounge for guests. Bemoaning the lack of poached haddock at the breakfast table and satisfying ourselves with the only breakfast stuff seemingly designed to look exactly like a pair of hastily removed ladies panties, namely the Croissant, we settled the not inconsiderable bill and left. This was supposed to be a cheap and cheerful trip, but we were having such a good time and the pre-requisite tally-ho demeanour could only be maintained by spending a few bob.

The final stage of the 1964 Monte Carlo Rally was a street stage, essentially the same circuit used by today's Formula 1 race. There was a complex handicap system in place and, in order to claw back the lead, Ljungberg's Falcon had to beat Hopkirk's Mini by more than half a minute around Monaco.

I love to compare before and after photographs, so a trip to the Grand Hotel hairpin gave an indication of how tight this place was for the big Fords (pic above). It was time for us to drive. We fought heavy heads and readied our MINI on the start–finish line on Le Boulevard Albert 1er—I am not going to confess to humming Fleetwood Mac's 'The Chain' in writing here—before stamping on the gas and tearing through the traffic up to the Sainte-Dévote corner, named after the Patron Saint of Monaco and Corsica. Scattering tourists, we cornered hard and up the hill, past new money vulgarities at Versace and into Casino Square. Hopkirk wouldn't have paused here, and neither did we, especially given a previous financial contretemps. Right, left, right and we were down the narrow streets scything around suicidal moped riders, leather-faced lotharios in Russian-registered supercars and barely legal blondes carrying decorative dogs. The Grand Hotel hairpin has distinctive red and white kerbing outside to help racing drivers hit the perfect apex. We reluctantly gave way at the Portier traffic island before thundering into the tunnel.

There are few things as joyous as the sight of a police-manned radar trap facing the wrong way, and we barely lifted off as the MINI screamed past to hit a figure equating to the national speed limit x 3. Dr. O perked up, knowing that the next corner was Tabac, yet we were not here to stock up on stinking Gitanes and passed on three wheels as the MINI displayed that peculiarity of modern front-wheel-drive sports cars cornering at speed. At this spot in 1955, despite wearing his lucky blue helmet, Ascari crashed his Lancia into the harbour. Our speed dropped off and we wound our way round to La Rascasse, the final corner, and the finish. As I wondered how our lap time compared to that of Hopkirk's, I was met with a stout tap on the window, and was obliged to attend the police station on Quai Antoine to endure a lengthy and humourless lecture by a pedantic officer with a sub-GCSE grasp of the Queen's English.

Hopkirk, as we now know, had held off the 5.7 litre Falcon in his 1 litre Mini for the most famous of wins. Today, he does tremendous work for charity and is as modest about his achievements as one would expect of a true gentleman. His co-driver, Liddon, sadly died in a plane crash in the colonies in 1987, a thought at the forefront of my mind as Dr. O and I packed ourselves aboard the easyJet flight back to Luton.

Zandvoort

Car;   Toyota Yaris. A four-word car review of
            the thing; boring, boring and boring.

Location;   Zandvoort circuit, The Netherlands.

Duration;   Half an hour of happy lapping.

Styled by the Japanese and built by the French. When it comes to cars, the Yaris is arse-about-face to me. I'd rather have people playing to their strengths; the French doing the creative stuff and the Japanese screwing them together. Still, the little Toyota is a popular choice for oldies and a predictable sight in the car rental car stable My flight landed at Schipol airport, Amsterdam. If I were to match the perfect car for my intended destination on this trip, I would have had a March 731, the F1 car of a racer who had always fascinated me; Roger Williamson. Instead, I got a Yaris.

Roger Williamson was born and raised, like me, in Leicestershire. The wealthy owner of Donington Park, Tom Wheatcroft, took a shine to him and funded Williamson through the lower formulae of racing, where he was pretty successful. I know an old boy who raced karts against Williamson early in his career and he had not a bad word to say about him. What he would have made of the Yaris, a car whose doors close with a *spang*, we will never know, for Williamson died in a horrendous accident at Zandvoort in 1973. I wanted to see the place, to get a feel for it. Road trips should have a reason and this was mine.

The story goes that the Mayor of Zandvoort, during the war, convinced the local Nazi commander to rebuild the seafront by telling him he ought to have a nice promenade to have a victory parade on after the war. Hitler only had one ball, a bridge too far, Churchill etc. etc. and as we now know, the Allies won. The Mayor of Zandvoort had a nice new seafront and amongst the dunes lay the foundations of a brilliant circuit for motorsport. Trackdays are occasionally held here but it's prohibitively expensive for me, for some reason, and it would mean the usual faff of dragging my own rotbox across the Continent at huge expense to revisit the scene of my hero's grisly death. You've read the cover; this is about rental cars. Like the boring Yaris.

I only intended to visit. It was closed. I drove the perimeter of the circuit hoping for a better view of the track hidden in the undulating dunes and then, at the end of the straight, was a wide open access gate. I sat there, in the Yaris, looking like a lost pensioner. I got out. No noise. No people. A couple of hundred metres down the straight, on the right, I could see the pit lane and control buildings. I waited some more. Seagulls and silence. Williamson overturned his March, a fairly ordinary accident by the standards of the time, but his car caught fire and he was trapped beneath his burning car. His friend, David Purley (of the LEC fridges business) immediately stopped his own car and snatched a fire extinguisher from a hapless marshal. He too was burned trying to overturn Williamson's car as racers ignored the horror and barely let up as they passed. I was always touched by the helplessness of the situation, Purley's bravery and the sheer terror of a man burning to death as people stood by.

I had to complete Williamson's lap. I knew the direction of the track and that it was closed, so I decided to trespass. The March was powered by a Ford Cosworth DFV V8 with at least 400 bhp. The Yaris had a 70 bhp noise-maker up front and very, very little to commend it. I let out the clutch and nailed it, spinning the wheels and joined the circuit. I didn't get far at all. I recall spotting a short woman with a clipboard running onto the track at the precise moment the engine faltered, not realising I'd hit the limiter in 3rd and wondering how she'd managed to remotely cripple my car. She was going mental. Utterly mental. I stopped but locked the doors, which seemed to make her even more mental. I put the window down an inch and tried to apologise. An English accent usually seems to get me out of trouble abroad but it didn't help much here. Eventually, I unlocked the door and she got in the passenger seat. She knew about Roger Williamson and that was why, rightly, she was angry about my intrusion. It wasn't safe to gatecrash a track. She calmed down a bit when she realised I was trying to pay tribute, albeit in a sodding Yaris, to a hero of mine. She said it would not be safe to reverse on track, even though the place was empty, and (perhaps in sympathy) allowed me to complete my lap.

The first corner of Zandvoort is named Tarzan. Apparently, a local who had a vegetable garden would only sell his parcel of land to the circuit builder if they allowed him to name the corner. And he liked Tarzan. It's a brilliant corner to race on because it is heavily cambered, allowing you to charge around, banked, barely letting up. I was told to slow down. The surface is good, it dips and falls, like a rollercoaster rhythm. It's a wonderful place to drive, even in a bastard Yaris.

"Complete the lap" she said, "then off!" I knew the circuit layout and devised a plan in my head. Apologising again for trespassing and apologising for not speaking Dutch, I asked the name of the fourth corner. "Rob Slotermakerbocht" came the begrudging reply. I asked how to pronounce it and then spent the next nine corners spitting on the inside of the windscreen trying to master this mouthful of Dutch. Speed was creeping up again. "Rob Slotermakerbocht!" she shouted over the engine. Then turn 13. What's this one, then? "Arie Luyendijkbocht". What? "ARIE LUYENDIJKBOCHT!" Very slowly, mouthing each lump of this name, I repeated it over and over, trying to master it as my speed crept up. She shouted at me: "ARIE GOD-DAMN LUYEN-DIJK-BOCHT!" and I overshot the pit entrance. We would have to go round again. I am so sorry, I said. I was distracted trying to pronounce Arie... how do you say it again?

I had completed Roger Williamson's lap. And three more, the next ruse being to ask my angry co-driver to take my photo with my camera phone which was broken, and the final time of driving too fast and accidentally missing the exit due to "really needing a wee". There's a statue of Roger Williamson at Donington Park. David Purley later came unstuck in a stunt plane accident. I was, very nearly, battered to death by a little Dutch lady with a clipboard.

Col de la Bonette: Europe's highest road?

Car;   Rented Hyundai i30.

Location;   Col de la Bonette.

Duration;   24 hours plus flights there and back.

"He's six foot high, with the body of an athlete by Praxiteles, and a face, oh incredible, the mystery of Botticelli, the refinement and delicacy of a Chinese print, the youth and piquancy of an unimaginable English boy." Me? No, of course not. This is what writer and homosexual sadomasochist, Lytton Strachey, said of George Mallory, the man who may or may not have been the first to conquer Everest. Mallory, when asked why he wanted to reach the summit of the world, simply said "because it's there". Putting myself and one of England's greatest adventurers in the same paragraph might seem pompous, but with 24 hours and a hundred quid budget, my challenge seemed perhaps vaguely comparable. I wanted to conquer Europe's highest road—just because it's there. In a rented hatchback.

The Col de l'Iseran was originally, at 2770 m, Europe's highest paved through road. The Col de la Bonette reached 2715 m. For reasons shrouded in the mists of time, around 1961, the locals wanted their road to be higher and built a superficial loop around the peak of Bonette, taking it to 2802 m. Today, the few people who bother to drive up there will take the original road, not bothering with the extra kilometre or so around the volcanic peak of Cime (peak) de la Bonette, which reaches 2802 m, making it Europe's highest through road. There are other, even higher, roads elsewhere on the map, but these are dead ends. Mallory would have pushed a

Hyundai off the mountainside rather than three-point-turn it.

It was unfinished business for me. On a previous trip to this area, we had been thwarted by snowfall and had abandoned our ascent of this pass. Large steel gates and signs close the road off in inclement weather and it's not unusual for the road to be completely closed from November to May, due to heavy snowfall. The locals might have cheated a bit when it comes to having the highest road in the Alps (and, therefore, Europe), but they don't seem phased by the terrain. I had flown into Nice, as before, and driven up through the Mercantour National Park, ever higher, on the D64 road.

There's nothing much wrong with a Hyundai i30 but, as medics will know, altitude sickness symptoms can start to occur at 1500 m above sea level, about the same altitude as trees stop growing. Something I passed miles back. At 2400 m and higher, symptoms resembling flu, carbon monoxide poisoning or a hangover can take hold. This is altitude sickness. The car was gutless before and felt oxygen-starved down on the Med coast but by 2500 m, it was really wheezing. The few locals I encountered seemed to drive like utter psychopaths, rushing from one tiny hamlet to the next. It became a challenge to hold them off for as long as possible, submit to the inevitable overtake, then hang on to them for as long as I possibly could .The terrain, above the treeline, is harsh. Looking down, I saw pleasant grassy meadows with the odd shepherd. There's ibex here and marmots, too. Above are birds on the breeze and grey scree, jagged peaks and skies which seem so clear and close and yet capable of dumping God knows what weather on you on a whim.

Citroen Visas, Peugeot 205 vans and other Gallic peasant transport rules up here. In white, mostly, with rust scabs and wood or agricultural things tied to the roof with rope. They seem to have long-travel suspension and lean around the corners to enable them to vanish up a pass far quicker than the Hyundai could.

There are few cash barriers up here. The dark grey gravel that seems to form most of the scenery is shoved into a rudimentary kerb, beyond which there's a near-vertical mountainside to whatever lies below. The kerb is about 20–30cm tall, at best. As I wound my way up the mountainside, I assessed it for impact resistance. I reckoned maybe 30–40mph would be enough to bulldoze it out of the way. Unlike other Alpine passes, there are plenty of places where you can build up a bit of speed here, even on the way up. It's not Pikes Peak, but pikey's peak in a rented car and little time to hit the top. As it snakes its final turn, the D64 nips through a break in the

jagged hillside on the right and straight on is the C1, a tiny
road that runs around the peak. The highest road. And on
the long right-hander, there's a stone marking the
summit. It celebrates the opening of the road in 1961,
refers to the Route Napoléon and the Nice to Briançon
road, and talks of national defence.

There is no one here. The clouds, not far above, seem to
dampen the few sounds I make, like kicking the door shut
of my donkey of a car. There's a short dirt path to the
peak itself. I am not that unfit, but scrambling up I am
quickly out of puff. The cold air is biting. I look down on
the car, on the mountains and it is so beautiful. It's calm,
silent and remote. It's the highest point on the roads of
Europe but only a quarter as high as Everest. I slither back
to the car, heater on. I start the car but, for whatever
reason, forget I had left it in gear. The car leaps forward
30 cm, steering on full lock, nose over the edge. The

gravel catches me. Pants shat, I calm my nerves and head off.

There's insufficient time to get back to Nice that day, my 24-hour rental expires at midday the following day, so I head for a hotel I had booked. Staying in the mountains, off-season, means it's cheap. The Hotel l'Ecureuil caters for the skiing crowd and the owner is overly friendly. He asks me what I'm doing here, so I explain. He asks, in Franglais, if I would leave a positive review on TripAdvisor for him. I did so and you can still find it on TripAdvisor. It reads as follows:

"Nice simple rustic Hotel, the nearest decent to the base of Col de la Bonnette, typical alpine furnishings, friendly service and fair prices. Good food. The col de la Bonnette is open for a few months each summer and at 2802m high is well worth a hoon (see picture). Look out for the Marmots though, they're great for a bit of no strings attached holiday shenanigans, but before you know it

they're on the blower at 2am in tears claiming to be up the duff..."

Superheroes go barnstorming

Car;   Tipo 250. Not the boxy Fiat hatchback but
              a perfect homage to the Maserati 250F.

Location;   An airfield in England with abysmal
              security and a very lax attitude to HSE.

Duration;   Half a glorious day.

You know when you see kids toddling around with
Superman outfits on, or a tea-towel cape, oblivious to
how they might look and quite convinced in their mind
that they *are* a superhero? When you slip on a vintage
leather helmet and goggles and sit in a car like this, you
feel just as convinced. You are superhero. You are Fangio.
The Maserati 250F is the most beautiful and iconic
Formula 1 car of all time. In 1957, Fangio drove one at the
Nürburgring, where he overcame a 48-second deficit in 22
laps, passing the race leader on the final lap to take the
most famous of wins. In doing so, he broke the
Nürburgring lap record ten times. If you want one today,
you'll need a million quid or more, unless you're on good
terms with Andy at Tipo250.co.uk, who built this fantastic
machine. He's a mate of mine.

The Tipo 250 is not some calamitous kit car or rough-
around-the edges recreation; it is a painstakingly
researched and meticulously built evocation of the real
thing. Like the Maserati, it has a 2.5 litre straight six
engine fed by three Weber carburettors, period tyres and
unassisted brakes. OK, so the engine is actually from a
BMW and the exhaust manifold is on the wrong side, but
when you look very closely, you'll find the option of
headlights and discrete mudguards, which means this

glorious machine is somehow road-legal. Which got me thinking...

What do you compare this beautiful car to? You may as well benchmark it against Kelly Brook's cleavage or a vintage biplane. Kelly is currently playing hard to get (blasted restraining order), but I did know a man with a biplane who is game. The Tiger Moth is a two-seat ex-RAF trainer that taught Spitfire pilots the basics, a thing of string, wood and wonder. Designed in 1931, it has no airspeed indicator other than a metal spring on the wing that bends with speed, pointing at guestimate numbers applied by pen. It smells of oil, avgas and superheroism, and belongs to my mate Will, who can be scrambled at a moment's notice.

So, to play at superheroes, we went barnstorming. Utilising a disused runway and taking a very liberal interpretation of the Highway Code, most of the Road

Traffic Acts, the law regarding trespass and CAA rules, we met at an ungodly hour at a secret location in England. Do not ask me where. I'm not sure I could ever find it again anyway. I primed the Tipo 250. I didn't do this stunt with a view to making a film or selling a story, and any thoughts of eventually writing a book weren't even remotely on my horizon. I had access to the car, knew a guy with a plane and was told that if I bought twelve bacon sandwiches (brown sauce on six, ketchup on six), then the security at this site would (and I quote them directly here) "f*ck off for a couple of hours so you can kill yourselves".

The cockpit of the car has been built to suit Andy of Tipo's 6'3" frame and not my scrawny arse. The gear change is on my right and I felt precariously perched, despite sitting in a steel tubular spaceframe chassis. Fangio was nicknamed "El Chueco", the bow-legged one, and I can imagine his his posture would have been more appropriate sat astride this machine than my own frame. I had to think hard about how to drive it. The vintage rubber has only a small contact patch. The large three-spoke steering wheel is wood-rimmed. The last wheels (legally) on this greasy, pitted mile of tarmac were those of Wellington bombers a very long time ago. I could not afford to crash this car and there are lumps of rubble everywhere.

There was no complex timing gear, no comms equipment and I had been prevented from stealing a few cones from the roadworks on the A1 en route by over-protective workmen. We were alone. The Tiger Moth moves so slowly. It hangs in the air with the dull drone of an ancient 130 horsepower Gipsy Major engine pulling it along at a speed barely sufficient to generate enough lift on those fabric-clad wings to cheat gravity. It's beautifully ungainly and looks like it shouldn't work. The Tipo 250, on the other hand, stands up to the old motorsport adage "if it looks right, it is right". The gearbox snicked into first with my right hand and I gently pulled away. It is easy to get moving, visibility is good as you sit so high, the car starts to roll. The plane approaches, much lower than I thought, causing me to involuntarily duck as it wails overhead. I can clearly see Will, smiling. In his head, he is a Spitfire pilot. I am Fangio.

He banks, hanging in the air, I use the full width of the airstrip and a little bit of turnip field to get the car facing the right way. It's no surprise that there were so many fatalities in the Maserati's heyday. The seating position feels so lofty it accentuates the narrow track and makes those tyres seem even thinner too. If it goes over, which they did a bit, it's all on your neck. I could not afford to do this. Andy's coach-making skills gave those lovely rivets, the perfectly curved panels and the same stance as the original vintage racer. Here comes the plane again.

Will seemed to want to go even lower. The amount of noise the Tiger Moth creates does not translate to speed. It floated alongside the 250 for a hundred yards or so as we tried to match speed, shouting encouragement into the wind as we raced along. Barnstorming was created between wars when a surplus of obsolete military aircraft came onto the market. Out-of-work pilots would fly across America, buzzing little towns and inviting them to pay to watch car versus plane races like this. Notable barnstormers include famous aviators such as Charles

Lindbergh and Hermann Göring. Lesser known names were no less courageous or interesting. These include Frenchman Roland Georges Garros (the victor in the first air battle in history when he brought down a Zeppelin by *crashing into it*), Bessie Coleman (the first female pilot of African American descent, killed when a stray spanner fell into her engine), Clyde Edward 'Upside-Down' Pangborn and wing-walker Lillian Boyer. Look these people up; they are amazing.

I did not want an audience but there were heads popping up on the other side of the hedge and our commotion had caused cars to stop. I got the impression Will wanted a word as he was waving from the cockpit. Then, against all logic, he brought it in to land and I was so distracted I drove into a field. The surface was cratered, concrete broken, huge weeds and litter blew across the filthy surface. As the Tiger Moth taxied between the rocks and rubble, I could hear a terrible grinding noise and suspected a mechanical mishap. But it was the tailwheel, or lack of wheel, the design not having one—a sprung bit of wood keeps the tails off the deck, albeit noisily. "Some more?" grins Will. God, yes, as soon as I've dug this car out. I am Fangio.

The acceptable face of green laning

Car;   Borrowed Volvo Laplander, Vogn, felt, 1/2
               tonn, 4x4, Volvo, modell L3314N, as the
               Norwegian Army call it.

Location;   Some scenery, Norway.

Duration;   A day to Ryanair up there, a day charging
about in it.

When a friend of mine, Bjørn, invited me to see his latest
purchase, I nearly declined. A masochistic approach to
motoring means that his previous purchase was an old
Freelander (scrapped) and the one prior to that was
another old Freelander (scrapped). Now, I don't mind
smuggling Land Rover parts up to Norway now and then
to help keep Bjørn on the road, but I'm not swallowing
another condom full of head gaskets for *anyone*.
Fortunately, his latest 4x4 was something far more
acceptable. In fact, it is bloody brilliant. It's a Volvo
Laplander and I was itching to try it.

I flew up there. Blagging a go in something so unlike anything I'd driven before, on lanes I wouldn't attempt on horseback, looked like fun. Green laning, in the UK, seems to be the sort of activity enjoyed primarily by middle-aged men in camouflage who smell like a beermat. Bjørn is nothing like that. He is a fruit loop though. Launched in 1961 for the Swedish Army, the Laplander is a simple 4×4 sitting on leaf springs and powered by the same 82bhp B18 engine also found in the Volvo Amazon. The bodywork is welded 3 mm steel and the whole shebang weighs c.1600 kg. This is the Pltgbil model. I have no idea how to pronounce that, nor what it means, but it's Swedish so, therefore, it is cool. With the canvas top and windscreen folded down, it'll fit in the back of a cargo plane. This example was mechanically excellent and cosmetically battered. White spots inside are daylight coming in through holes in the bodywork. Inside the cockpit is a metal cover over the engine which can be accessed on the hoof and a skinny, bus-flat steering wheel. It's a cab-forward design, with the brake pedal wedged against the steering column and brakes that will only rub a smidgen of speed off, when going slowly, uphill, while simultaneously clutching at passing scenery with your bare hands. The steering feels like you have prosthetic arms and are arm-wrestling a drunken bear.

There are levers for diff control. I don't know what that means. We had a few beers as we hadn't caught up in ages. Then a few more beers when we had. Drink driving on public roads, in Norway, is punishable by prison. No mucking about. I had some idea that green lanes were maybe not public highways and no copper could get his car down the lane after us, but Bjørn's technique was far more direct. Out of his barn, he said, straight across a ploughed field and arrow-straight flat out into the woods opposite—this is not a public road. The owner of the farmland had done his stint for drink driving and had lost his licence, but because he's a farmer, he's still allowed to drive his tractor.

It burst into life, very, very noisily. There's a certain technique needed to drive it. Bjørn explained it not before we set off, but when we were already hurtling downhill over furrowed mud. The brakes are mainly for decorative purposes and steering should be attempted a few hundred metres before you might actually need to change direction. It's actually much quicker than you might think and, not stressing about collecting any stone chips, I twatted through the undergrowth, eventually emerging from the forest with great pace at precisely the point a family had been enjoying a picnic. Across overgrown fields and a children's playground to squeals of laughter (me, not them), I managed to rein in the Laplander just before we ended up in the fjord. Bjørn reckons these might float. I didn't want to try. Behind us, we had punched a hole in the scenery in a perfect square shape, the silhouette of the Volvo.

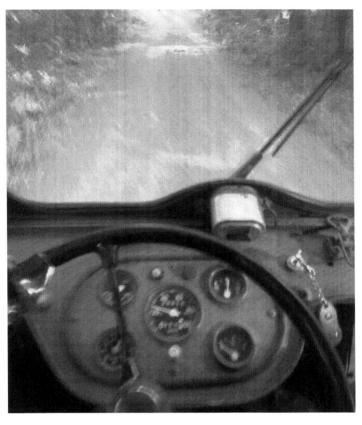

This was *honestly* the most fun on wheels I've had in ages. It may seem like oikish behaviour, but the Laplander is the acceptable face of green laning. It's no-nonsense. There's no pretence, no 'lifestyle' connotations, no silly image, no 'one life live it' rubbish and no head gasket worries. You can reliably chart your own road through the scenery at random. Kids point and laugh and grown-ups smile, even when you drive through their picnic. Only Volvo could create something like the Laplander.

We stopped to remove a few stray saplings from the wheel arches and had another beer, then hauled it round in the direction of home and punched another route through the pines and birch trees. Certain Laplanders came with an anti-tank gun fitted on the back. We agreed to upgrade it for the next trip and shoot a few Freelanders to bits.

Monte Carlo and bust

Car;   Rented Renault Twingo. Not found
              outside France much for good reason.

Location;   Nice airport, Col de Turini, Col de la
              Cayolle and Barcelonnette, France then
              Monaco.

Duration;   24 hours abroad plus flights there and
              back.

If you want something enough, you *can* find a way to justify it; just apply some man maths and away you go. In this case, the 'something' was a trip similar to my Stelvio trip and my man maths calculation went as follows : (*easyJet + rental car + €20 to reduce insurance excess to zero x 24 hours*) < (*Eurotunnel + 3000 km drive + inevitable damage to my own car x 4 days*).

easyJet from Stansted to Nice is simple enough, collecting a car when wearing a T-shirt with the logo 'NOTHING HANDLES LIKE A RENTAL' less so. With hindsight, we must have looked like a stag do gone wrong, but after downgrading from a Ka to a Twingo, Dr. O and I escaped Nice airport followed by a ragtag bunch of fellow man mathematicians with real names I cannot reveal due to a superinjunction, or something. Destination; Monte Carlo, via some serious scenery.

We stopped at the foot of Col de Turini to fit some VBOX
cameras to the Twingo. Mr. Tipex stopped to apply some
vinyl stripes to his own rental car, instantly turning it into
a hot Gordini version. Gordini used to make genuinely hot
versions of little Renaults. Today, the name is used to flog
go-faster stripes. The Col de Turini runs up rather
overgrown mountainsides, meaning that you focus on the
endless switchbacks, instead of gawping at the distant
Med. The roads were deserted and the VBOX recorded a
vmax of 46 mph on this 'stage', a little way short of the
WRC boys, but they aren't saddled with 75 bhp of
screaming French diesel. The peak is 1607 m, a mile high,
and noticeably colder than the coast. After a quick stop
for coffee, we headed further inland.

Next up was the Col Saint Martin. Slightly faster roads, still climbing, past some impressive old gun emplacements which seemed to be facing the opposite direction to Germany for reasons best known to French military tacticians. We only saw one other car up there, a UK-plated Elise steaming past us the other way. Steaming as in driven quickly, not steaming as in K-series failure, for the record.

Our original plan had been to attempt the Col de la Bonette, Europe's highest road, a few metres higher than Stelvio. Unfortunately, it was closed due to snow, so we headed east and took the Col de la Cayolle that runs roughly parallel to it, and at 2326 m, nearly a kilometre higher than the mountain we'd just driven up.

At this point, TomTom's optimistic ETA at our hotel for the night was exposed as pure electronic fantasy. When the total distance to the destination is nearly three times the distance as the crow flies, you know you're in for some switchbacks, and so it proved. Dr. O and I taking it in turns to drive hard and make each other honk, climbing utterly deserted mountain roads, understeering into every hairpin and smoking the tyres out of them.

The summit of Col de la Cayolle was postcard-perfect, but as the temperature plummeted (20 degrees C colder than when we left Nice) and the light started to fail, we barely had time to stop.

Above the treeline and with snow almost encroaching on the road, the early start and hard driving started to take their toll. It is tiring to drive enthusiastically in such conditions. The final descent into Barcelonnette was a fast drive on a single lane road down a steep-sided canyon, over tiny bridges with 90-degree approach angles, as the light faded and the 'Bond Themes' CD repeated itself for the third time that day. We made it in time for beers and a pizza topped with what the menu described as 'rape cheese'.

After another early start, the cars were looking almost as knackered as we were. We couldn't hang about though. After the previous day playing at WRC drivers, we were off to Monte Carlo to play at being F1 drivers. Back up the Col de la Cayolle as the sun rose over the mountains was mesmerising, so mesmerising that we nearly had a head-on with startled looking gendarmerie driving a police car the other way on the single track road. If that wasn't enough, we nearly collected a bonnet ornament in the form of a large animal that looked like a cross between an otter and Sandi Toksvig.

Over the peak, we stopped for a group photo, at which point the Twingo's dash illuminated with 'le spanneur electronique de la merde', and refused to start as the other guys smoked off down the valley without us.

After some swearing, we finally got on the move, our route helpfully marked by bits that had fallen off the other cars. There is no way I would want to risk my own P&J in these mountains. The scenery may have been a geologist's wet dream, but lumps of granite are to tyres what hot coals are to bare feet, and you're a long way from help up there.

Driving down the Gorges de Daluis, with tight one-way tunnels cut into the red rock mountainside, we came across Billy and his mate who were struggling with a crippled three-wheeled Fiesta. Shortly afterwards, we caught up with the rest of the group, who were struggling to extinguish their VW Polo. The other cars were equally ugly: a Ford Ka that had been off-roading, another tatty Twingo like ours, a Peugeot 207 and a particularly hideous creation called a 'Peugeot 206 Plus', which is the old 206 with a 207's face grafted onto it. The cars, like sangria, that Greek dance and pedalos, were great in the sunny

Med, but you don't want to be doing them back in Blighty.

A liberal interpretation of the speed limits back to the coast found us entering Monte Carlo. My co-driver committed an act of road rage so funny that I laughed so much I nearly rear-ended a Porsche. In response to a local with no road manners, he adopted a faux-frog accent, opened a window and shouted "Ferk you! You an' your 5 brozzers make zer sex with zer tortoise! AT ZER SAME TIME!" I was crying with laughter. The driver who had cut us up was confused and trying to reply in French. He was interrupted by my mate who continued, "and when it 'ibernate, you tempt 'im out with a lettuce leaf, and when 'e stick 'is 'ead out, YOU STICK YOUR DICK IN 'IS FACE". I have no idea where this bestial gibberish came from but it was so funny and a great way of diffusing a bit of potential unpleasantness on the most pleasant of streets of Monte Carlo. The names Monaco and Monte Carlo are often confused (and often by me). Monaco is the country (strictly speaking, a principality), which has four quarters,

Monte Carlo being one, the others being Fontvieille, Monaco-Ville and La Condamine.

We had intended to meet in Casino Square, but the top-hatted concierge waved us on, so we parked up in the harbour and, for a glorious moment, pretended we were obscenely wealthy and owned one of the massive yachts. With the Monaco GP due to start shortly, the barriers and grandstands were all in place, so with Murray Walker in my head, I set off for a few laps. Dodging the hypercars and mopeds was challenging enough, but a bejewelled über-cougar being dragged onto the track, sorry, road, by an inbred dog really dented my progress. Lewis doesn't have this trouble. Despite hitting 86 out of the famous tunnel (kph, sadly, not mph), my best effort was just under nine minutes. The whole circuit is incredibly narrow, with turns like the Grand Hotel hairpin being challengingly tight in a Twingo, let alone a Grand Prix car.

As always, there were some awesome cars on display; sadly, none of them will ever be used to anything like their full potential. Outside the casino are supercars and luxury galore. I like to have a coffee and sit and watch those who take selfies; these people are as interesting as the machines themselves. I have never understood selfie culture. If you want your picture with a Ferrari, why not just visit the showroom? Monte Carlo (Monaco, whatever) is a place for poseurs. A white McMerc SLR with Russian plates driven by a leather-faced lothario with a barely legal blonde in the passenger seat kind of summed the place up. Nice to visit, but a day is enough of this nonsense. The hills above had been more fun.

€43 of gazole filled the Twingo, we gave the mostly broken cars back to the bemused rental office staff, checked in and flew home. My maths teacher once told me that I would never amount to anything in life, but I reckon I get an A+ in man maths.

Skipping school with junior

Car;   Mazda MX-5 mk 1, 1.6 litre. My own car
                  for over a decade, with a decades' worth
                  of neglect under the bonnet.

Location;   Curborough circuit, England.

Duration;   "Junior will be off school for one day for a
                  dental appointment."

I've met the headmaster. He's an insipid little ginger
fellow who drives a Ford Kuga. I'm not gingerist by the
way; I'm just painting a picture here. As the head of my
daughter's school, I ought to treat him with more respect,
but in the reception is one of those awful motivational
posters: "Pupils with the highest attendance rates
typically get the best results", that sort of thing. The
reason for my prickly tone when describing this school is
that the teachers are often on strike, putting a hole in the
head's 'attendance = results' argument. Also, it's the
same school I occasionally attended in the 1980s, when
striking seemed to be a national pastime. It is not a good
school and it seems there's not much I can do about it. If
this opening paragraph was a letter to the head about the
non-attendance of my daughter, it would simply read "ur
school is shit, we gone racing m8".

I ought to elaborate on the use of the word 'racing' here;
sprints are timed laps of a short and technically
challenging circuit. One car is on the track at a time and
you're racing the clock, not other lumps of metal.
Curborough circuit can be rented fairly cheaply by the day
and a friend of mine runs a popular little sprint series
throughout the year. They're cheap events because they
are commonly held mid-week. That means school time.

PE in a wet field with a sadist, followed by English taught by someone who doesn't have English as their first or even second language, then a spot of compulsory passive smoking at lunchtime, topped off with an afternoon of occasional bullying ignored by yet another supply teacher. Or a day racing. I didn't have to ask her twice.

You'll note that I am not naming my daughter here. Not that I mind the school knowing what we get up to. I'm quite proud of her achievements at school and on track actually, but I wouldn't want to jeopardise her chances of getting a driving licence. At the time the events in this chapter happened, she was just 11, although perhaps driving a Bentley Continental when she was 13 is a bigger crime. This time we were in my Mazda MX-5 mk 1, a very early car which usually requires a bit of bodging to get it moving in the morning. Her first memory is of this car. I recall taking her for a drive, sat on a coat (her, not me) and stopping to take a photo. She remembers this moment; I think she would have been about 2 or 3 years old. Anyway, we made it as far as the A5 before having to stop to replace a snapped belt, and we arrived at Curborough circuit in time to miss the safety briefing and sign-on, which was convenient as junior wouldn't have a licence for another six years at least.

She is very tall. With a helmet on, and wearing sunglasses, she could easily pass for someone in their late teens, even then. Which is good, because children aren't supposed to drive here. We walked around the circuit, me explaining what happens, when and where, to familiarise ourselves with the way a sprint works. There is always some interesting machinery in the paddock. Sprint events cater for different classes, so you'll have everything from the kid in the stripped out Saxo (which go very well on sprints, incidentally) to professionals with single-seaters giving their car a shakedown. Everyone is always genuinely friendly and happy to chat; there's lots of interesting spannering going on and cups of tea to be shared. Junior was told to keep schtum in case we got rumbled and we were almost caught out when she asked if there was an ice cream van.

CBA. Not just the acronym for 'can't be arsed', but clutch, brake, accelerator. It comes naturally to drivers with a few miles under their belt but junior still needed reminding. Helmet on, keep quiet, sit in the queue to get on track. Gate open, a 'GO' from the marshal and we're off. She didn't stall and we piled into the first right-hander, then built up speed in 2nd to the Molehill corner, clipping the kerb neatly, then a long opening right-hander onto the straight. At this point, she is already going too fast and we have a shouted argument about it. She wins the argument by ignoring my advice on the braking point, which she got away with on the first lap but not the second and we overcook it a bit. Round we go, figure of eight, the Mazda's coarse-sounding twin cam engine screaming. I do not recall her time. I do recall us both laughing like maniacs.

Motorsport employs around 40,000 people in the UK, according to the Internet. It encourages the use of maths, physics and materials technology. It also requires, if you're going to be any good at it, creativity. These are invaluable skills. Ask a child to solve an equation in a textbook, in a classroom, and you'll need more than a disinterested supply teacher to encourage the right results. Put that child in a car and encourage them to drive quicker, then, when their technique is good, they'll ask why the car won't go quicker. Then their brain really goes to work. What is 'power to weight ratio'? Why are brakes more important than power? How do we improve performance in those areas? There'll be someone in the paddock with oily hands who will have answers and ideas. They won't be asking why an 11-year-old has skipped school. Skiving and sprints should be on the school curriculum. I ought to tell that headmaster, but junior now attends a better school.

Longbridge, and a scientific experiment

Car;	eBay-sourced Rover Metro 1.1 Quest. Hydragas = laughing gas.
Location;	Cowley (England) to Casablanca (Morocco).
Duration;	Five days one way, by car.

Those who enjoyed my last book, "Confessions from quality control", might want to skip this chapter, as it was originally included there. Those who missed it might want to read on, or perhaps just enjoy the picture of a monkey eating the security manual of our Longbridge lovely.

The very name, Longbridge, seems to conjure up images of mass industrial action. We've all heard tall stories such as cars being built with brake discs on one side and brake drums the other. I read somewhere that they supposedly lost half a dozen cars a week due to theft—people somehow just drove them off-site. In one infamous strike in their darkest days, £10 million worth of productivity was lost due to a dispute over staggering tea break times. Sadly, I never had any dealings with Longbridge myself, other than to once work with an oik of an ex-QA engineer whose party piece was to drop his trousers, stuff his genitals between his legs, bend over and shout "*fruitbowl!*" I was told he was one of their best guys. MG today sometimes finishes off Chinese-built cars there, but it's a skeleton staff compared to the 25,000 that once worked there.

I really wanted to see if Longbridge's products were as bad as many would have you believe—it had long gnawed away at me. Now, working in another industry, I no longer had access to the measurement equipment needed for an accurate assessment of their build quality, and, of course, MG Rover hadn't built a new car in a decade. In 2014, I colluded with a few fellow motoring masochists and came up with a plan. We would buy examples of 'industrial unrest Rovers' and put them to the test. Car manufacturers use rallying to demonstrate the durability of their cars and Formula 1 is considered the technical pinnacle of motorsport. For reasons that made perfect sense in the pub, we agreed to combine the Dakar Rally and the 1958 Casablanca Grand Prix circuit with a road trip to Morocco. I bought and collected a Rover Metro from a man in Nottingham. It was £299. The seller waved me off with a friendly warning: "*You do know these are sh*t, don't you?*" I wanted to find out for myself.

Setting off at half past bastard o'clock in the morning, my co-driver Darryl and I ragged down to Portsmouth in the Metro to meet fellow scientists Baz and Jimbo in their Maestro and Ben and Chas in their Rover 416; we boarded the ferry to Spain, and spent 24 hours clinging to the bar trying to put our paperwork in order. The nautical shortcut across the Bay of Biscay was stormy, yet I wasn't bothered that I hadn't put the handbrake on in the Metro—these cars were not coming back. I have an almost religious approach to prepping cars for road trips—if you replace just one rusty washer, you have to replace the nut, and then whatever it's holding... *ad infinitum* until you've done a full resto job. Changing one scabby connector upsets old wires and creaking circuits, setting off an endless chain of catastrophic maladies on a worthless car. I call it mechanical karma. Leave it all alone. They've managed 20+ years and only need to last a thousand miles more. I wanted to leave them as factory standard as possible, to see how well they were screwed together by the bolshie Brummies I'd heard so much about. We spent the maintenance budget on pith hats and stickers.

Spain was the easy part of the trip. Twenty-four hours of motorway to get down to the port in Algeciras for the crossing to Africa, a steady drive for the cars. Yet, at the first hill coming out of Santander, the Maestro overheated and broke down. It was the first time I had a chance to look at the thing. When Rover stopped making the Maestro in Cowley, they sold unused parts to a company in Bulgaria who bodged a few together. Unsurprisingly, they didn't make as many as planned and sold the leftover bits back to a company in Ledbury, England, who assembled the car and sold it to buyers in the UK who were so keen to buy British that they'd accept an ancient design with a kph speedo, wrong-way wipers, Ox-cart comfort and a 1275 cc engine first built in 1951. They are, supposedly, rare and collectable now.

The overheating was traced to coolant that had never been changed, so we emptied the slurry from the rad, topped it up and went on our way. Driver Baz normally enjoys a Merc C63, so when he screamed over the radio *"Slow down! It's knackered! It has no power!"*, no one had any sympathy, not even startled Spanish traffic cops on the same frequency as our walkie-talkies. *¡Hola, amigos!* We arrived very late for the departure of the ferry to Morocco. Fortunately, the ferry was very *very* late and we made it in the nick of time. We waved goodbye to Europe and crossed the Strait of Gibraltar, arriving in Tangier, a few miles from Europe geographically but as far removed from civilisation as an overheating Maestro is from being stylish intercontinental transport.

Angry men in ill-fitting uniforms with guns shouted at us in French while locals hassled us. To get into Morocco, you have to complete a form to import yourself, another form to import your car, buy insurance for the car and then buy local currency, which we called 'stinkies' on account of their much-handled aroma. Much of the paperwork is in foreign (Arabic anyone?), it's hot, late and there's a jostling scrum of aggressively friendly locals clawing at your passport and wallet. Still, the cars had held up and we'd made it to Morocco. We headed south for an overnight stay in what the Internet had assured us was a clean, safe and friendly place just south of Tangier called Asilah. The Internet was wrong.

The hotel owner spoke some English and we got a four-bed, two-roomed apartment for £30. He was quite friendly until it came to being seen with us in public. He poked his head out of the door to first ensure it was safe before directing us to a nearby cat-infested restaurant for tagines, chips and olives. The cars were locked in a compound, next to a dead Renault 5 and a British-registered Mercedes G-wagon that looked utterly kaput. Leaving Asilah in the morning, we aimed to avoid the coastal motorway and give the cars a ragging on the old road that ran parallel to it, rally style. These roads are potholed, have crazy subsidence in places and the rain teemed down. We got lost. The Maestro conked out in an open sewer and as Baz was attempting to Google "Rover specialist near شارع الـ قرف الـ صـ يـ لة أصـ", it miraculously sprang back to life. Thank you, whoever made this car way back when, thank you.

Traffic is sparse on the open road but there is an incredible jumble of transport to be avoided in the towns. Motorbikes converted to pick-up trucks seemed popular, as well as Renault 4s and 5s, Peugeot 205s which also serve as taxis and smoky old Merc saloons with up to half a dozen people rammed in the back, all spewing pollution you could collect in a jar and sell as Moroccan Marmite. Our cars, though, were holding up surprisingly well. I'm not sure what I liked most about the Metro; it's incredible fuel economy, the boingy handling or the fact that we could drive it across Africa without worrying about the inevitable scrapes and scuffs suffered along the way. The Hydragas was saggy and the brake warning light was on, but "they all do that, sir". Hydragas is a brilliant invention and would work wonderfully on modern small cars on Britain's traffic-calmed, potholed roads, given another chance.

Owning a worthless Rover is fun. Ramming another worthless Rover at every opportunity in heavy traffic more so. The 416's back bumper took a dozen shunts to dislodge, but it isn't a Rover in the darkest, Longbridgist, Leylandist sense of the word. It's a leftover from Rover's collaboration with Honda. Japanese underpinnings with added wood cappings (crappings?), velour seats and an automatic gearbox, first owned by a doctor who paid more for the Nightfire Red paint option when new than Ben and Chas paid for the complete car. £180 gets you a reliable and comfortable car that, apart from vandalism by our fellow 'scientists' and the word TW*T inexplicably embroidered on a headrest by a previous owner, worked perfectly. Aside from the overheating A-series engine in the Maestro, all the cars were fine, if a bit battered, by the time we reached Casablanca. Our test hadn't quite covered the Paris–Dakar route, but we'd done a good enough chunk of it to know that our Longbridge-built Metro was perfectly reliable transport.

Stirling Moss won the Casablanca Grand Prix in 1958, a race organised by the King of Morocco to showcase his country. It's a blast down the coast road south of the city centre, then a rough left, left, left, left square back to the start. No faded colonial beauty here, nor Monégasque opulence, as the site of the original pit lane is now a KFC. The city is overcrowded and chaotic. Traffic is horrific. A blinkered population of five million on roads clogged with carts pulled by emaciated mules, overloaded lorries, mopeds and old French hatchbacks. We also saw a Rover 820 and a 618 and felt strangely envious of their luxury. We dumped the cars and took a taxi to dinner, whereupon our driver ran over a couple attempting to cross the road, backed up to get them from under his front wheels, then eventually dropped us at Rick's Café.

Of all the gin joints in all the world, why did we walk into this one? Rick's is brilliant. It's a bar and restaurant carbon-copied from the classic film *Casablanca*, run by an American ex-diplomat who serves the most fantastic food, cold beer and obligatory G&Ts. The decor is colonial splendor with Arab touches and a Sam on piano. It's beautiful and a complete contrast to the hellhole just outside the door. I was hoping for the company of Ingrid Bergmann but got Rover-owning Brits in flat caps and pith helmets enthusing about their cars.

The most BL of the lot was the Maestro. I expect that some readers may be unhappy that Darryl smashed in its doors and bonnet with a golf club when it overheated for the sixth time, but these cars, as rare as they now are, are worthless. If it was so special, why could we pick one up for the price of a few drinks at Rick's? We could only blame its unreliability on poor maintenance and the fact that Baz had zero mechanical sympathy. It certainly held together well. I think Jimbo had bonded with it but, like a holiday romance, it had to end. Ben and Chas had played a kind of BL Buckaroo with their 416. They claimed it was a reverse engineering project. They removed as many Rover parts as possible as they went along, arriving in Casa without most of its fake wood trim and superfluous luxury components, leaving mostly the Honda it was built on. But it got there, no fuss.

The Metro had just 41k on the clock and had been well maintained by a Nottingham pensioner, but watching a wing burst open like a bit of wet cardboard after a little collision with [*removed in case their insurer is reading this*], we decided that it needed about 200 kg of strengthening to make it safe, which would cripple the lightweight, chuckable feel that made it so much fun in the first place.

These cars might be a bit crap judged by modern standards, but we loved them and I'd like to think that the men of Longbridge who originally built them would approve of our experiment. And the results: after mistaking a mosque for a disco (I *thought* the music was rather peculiar), we retreated to the safety of the 14th floor of the Ibis, watched the chaos on the roads below and planned our retreat. Cars cannot be left in Morocco. Their import is tied to your own entry paperwork and passport, so they have to be exported and disposed of elsewhere. We trundled 250 miles to Tangier, past fields of miserable camels and gawping locals, and caught a late ferry back to Spain, which was overloaded and listing at a good 20 degrees when backing out into open water; a last bit of excitement from Africa.

We had a flight the following day but how to dispose of the cars, vaguely legally? They were worth less than a ferry ticket before we left; in their battered state, they're not worth the time or money to repatriate. We had tried to donate them to Oxfam. Oxfam didn't want them. The Maestro was left outside the gates of a Spanish scrapyard with the keys in it and the chaps piled into the other two cars. The Longbridge-built 416 and Metro crossed into Gibraltar, where we fed the cars' UK log books to the apes. We had tea and cake at a café and paid the elated waiter with the keys for both the Metro and the 416 parked outside, before jumping aboard a budget flight back home to cold, wet Brum.

Africa had been insane. We had only dipped our toe into the Dark Continent and each left two stone lighter with empty wallets and frayed nerves after just a few exciting days. I can think of no better destination for a Rover. There's a wonky Metro hubcap on my office wall and I'm only sad that I didn't repatriate the rest of it. So, the result of our experiment: they're all winners these cars. They did a trip that was considered beyond them by so many, stood up to the worst abuse we could chuck at them with zero maintenance or preparation and made us laugh. They have a battered, buggered and faded appeal that I've learned to appreciate. This road trip left me with a respect for Rover that I never had before.

Car vs. bike

Car;   Blagged Tiger Avon kit car. 280 bhp in
                  £280's worth of car, ish.

Location;   Leicester Speedway, England.

Duration;   Half a day.

Certain motoring subjects have been done to death in the pub. Audi vs. BMW, FWD vs. RWD and Peugeot vs. chemical castration (a tough one that). My ex-brother-in-law (hereafter known as EBIL) is a biker and when he was not recovering from multiple injuries, we often debated, over a pint, what is quicker, car vs. bike. I've never seen the appeal of dressing up like a Power Ranger and sitting on my scrotum with power I can't put down for fear of becoming an organ donor. I'd like to convey his side of this argument, but being as I'm writing this and not him, I won't. Some heated pub debates reach a clear conclusion outside in the car park, but we decided to settle this in a fair and scientific way instead, and have some fun too.

We agreed that we could each use any wheels of our choice and that the venue would be any convenient local circuit. I would fix the photographer and EBIL would fix the venue. Keeping in mind our usual haunts, Donington, Mallory and Cadwell, I was quite confident that my choice of wheels would spank his, regardless of venue. Following his directions, I ended up in Beaumont Leys, which, despite being a dog-rough suburb of Leicester, is famous only for its lighthouse*. I had bent the rules a bit and blagged a supercharged 280 bhp Tiger Avon on semi-slicks. I had driven Tigers before. They're a knock-off Caterham (having settled out of court, years ago, for the knocking off), offering sevenesque performance at a silly low price. The thing is, EBIL had bent the rules a bit too. The venue, he said, was Leicester's new speedway track.

I had never been to speedway before. The bikes have a four-stroke engine fuelled by methanol, no brakes and weigh about 80 kg. By using sprockets, the single gear ratio can be adjusted as required for the track conditions. Impressive, but it sounds like a lawnmower and I was still confident. EBIL had, just the previous day, popped a rib (again) and needed to call in a reserve. His stand-in was some whippet-faced lad with a Scandiwegian accent who is 'pretty handy' called Jan. Jan 'The Man' Gravesen. I Googled his name afterwards.

The track was empty, the photographers in place and a few loitering staff were grinning knowingly as I did a couple of laps alone to get a feel for the track. The surface is packed earth with a marbly gravel topping. Do you remember that Pirelli advert of a sprinter in stilettos "Power is nothing without control"? The Tiger lurched off, rear end waving about on the muck like a dog with worms, almost instantly you have to turn in for the first corner, get very sideways and try and point the car down the short straight before gently squeezing on the go pedal again. I stuck it in 2nd and left it there, concentrating on trying to get a feel for the scabrous surface beneath, while the Tiger seemingly wanted to turn around and do something else.

So, we lined up at opposite sides of the track, counted down 3, 2, 1 and just went for it. I hoped I could do the four laps before he caught me. I didn't even manage four corners. The roar of lawnmower announced he'd caught me and a faceful of cack confirmed he'd overtaken. I watched as he yanked the handlebars over and stuck out a boot to turn left. I followed the same line but couldn't keep up, there was no run-off for mistakes and the barriers were getting closer with attempts to go quicker. I tried point-and-squirt: the car pointed and I squirted in my jeans. Jan lapped me while I was still thinking about how to react. I then spotted that the inside line was rutted and tried grabbing some grip down there with the inside wheel and using less welly than before. This resulted in a tidier exit, less sideways shenanigans and quicker laps. Quick isn't always as much fun as though.

I had a breather, removed all the gravel from the cabin and re-thought my attack. With narrower front tyres and knobbly rears, I reckon the car would be much closer. It might make for an amusing spectator sport too, like a dirty drifting contest. Are there any motorsports that pitch cars directly against bikes? I'd pay to watch that. We went again. I couldn't get close to the bike. Someone else jumped in and had a go while I took pics and Jan kindly pebble-dashed my lens.

So, after dozens of laps, who won this contest? EBIL claimed victory in car vs. bike, but as I'm writing this and not him, I'll say I won. We had a huge laugh and thanked Leicester Speedway, Jan Gravesen and Tiger Racing for being such good sports. Making things like this happen calls for finding like-minded people with a disregard for the ugly details that would hamper such fun; risk assessment and insurance for example. People who know the risks, love the idea and are prepared to help make things like this actually happen because they, like me, bloody love this stuff. I can't thank them enough, even though I was picking gravel out of my holes for weeks afterwards.

Beaumont Leys Lighthouse, aka the police helicopter.

San Remo Grand Prix circuit

Car;	Rented MINI Cooper. Because no one would give me a Maserati.
Location;	Nice, France, then San Remo, Italy.
Duration;	24 hours plus flights there and back.

Anyone interested in motorsport will know Monaco. "A sunny place for shady people", someone once said. Someone with a better turn of phrase than what I've got. Amongst the apartment blocks housing tax exiles and around the harbour with moored up superyachts owned by iffy Russians run streets synonymous with Formula 1. Today, there is nowhere in the world with such a dazzling mix of glamour, opulence and motorsport history as Monaco. Yet, there once was. Half an hour's drive east along the dazzling Mediterranean coast, just over the border into Italy, sits the little town of Ospedaletti.

In 1937, there was a Grand Prix run on the impossibly tight streets of San Remo, as a one-off, and in 1947, there was a (non-championship) race for the first time just along the coast in Ospedaletti. The event retained the San Remo name. Ospedaletti was the venue for the official San Remo Grand Prix from 1948 to 1951. I haven't gotten to the bottom of why the racing ended in '51. Politics probably; this is Italy after all. The '51 race was eventful though. Johnny Claes' 4.5 litre Talbot suffered brake failure at speed on the main straight and he frantically waved at the crowd to move. The crowd cheerily waved back. Claes survived the accident but one person was killed, three seriously injured and many others hurt. Ascari won that race, the last at San Remo; he also won the first post-war race in '48, which is the one that most interests me. Before that though, a potted history lesson.

Prior to the Second World War, San Remo and Monaco were very similar; casinos, grand hotels, sunshine and the moneyed elite of Europe spending heavily. Monaco, during the war, was under the rule of Prince Louis II. Louis was born in Germany and was friends with the Vichy Government's Marshal Pétain. He sat on the fence during the war and the principality was occupied by (at various stages of the war) the Italians, the Germans and the Allies. Even the communists ran Monaco for a bit—imagine that today! My rather laboured point is that Louis's indecisive "we're allies with everyone and anyone" approach saved the town from receiving a pasting in the war. San Remo, in contrast, just over the border into Italy, was heavily bombed. As lovely as it is today, it never quite managed to recover like its more glamorous rival up the coast.

Enough history for now. I flew down to Nice with easyJet and picked up a MINI Cooper for another mental rental adventure. This was to be a quick trip. So there I was, lobbing enough coins at a tollbooth basket to get the barrier to open, not stopping to collect the €8.75 of loose change that missed, en-route to Ospedaletti. I had been in touch with a fantastic chap called Luca who had arranged to meet me at the Piccadilly corner at what was once the end of the main straight of the famous San Remo Grand Prix street circuit. Luca has an infectious enthusiasm, talks ten to the dozen and apologises endlessly for his 'bad English'. It's considerably better than my Italian. I rather like MINIs, although this one was an automatic convertible from Hertz's fun collection fleet. I had been hoping for a Maserati.

1948 was the year that San Remo held it's first official post-war Grand Prix. It also marked the racing return of Maserati and the first victory of F1 legend Alberto Ascari. There were other race entrants of note; Prince Bira of Siam, Baron Emmanuel de Graffenried of Switzerland and the 50-year-old pre-war ace Luigi Fagioli, all in Maserati 4CLs. Talbots, Delahayes and Simcas also featured, and a Ferrari 166SC driven by Raymond Sommer. The Ferrari was remarkable in that it was essentially a road car, yet it was raced successfully at San Remo and actually came 4th in '48. If only the Ferraris in Monaco today could be put to such good use. The Maserati cars, returning to racing for the first time since the war, were a development of an old 1930s design with a 1.6 litre four-cylinder supercharged engine. I made do with my 1.6 litre Cooper, sadly not a supercharged 'S'. I came here to lap this lovely old circuit. Time for the off.

With an enthusiastic Italian stood on the passenger seat pointing out various landmarks and looking like a tank commander whilst simultaneously taking photos and talking excitedly to his wife on his mobile, we set off. According to Luca's gesticulations, his wife was either morbidly obese or about to give birth. I didn't hang about. On the main straight is an old casino, now perhaps apartments, and next to that once stood the famous Hotel Regina. The hotel is now gone. "Bombed", said Luca, miming it too, for good measure. There's a sharp left here and the flat coast road turns up hill.

The terrain is very similar to Monaco; an ancient town clinging to a hillside. As soon as I'd rounded the Piccadilly corner, Luca told me to stop. We had a series of old photos and, as you might work out from the pictures, I tried to photograph the old picture in the modern setting so you can compare and contrast. To get the shot at Piccadilly, showing vintage Maseratis streaming up the hill, I had to park the MINI a bit illegally and climb the façade of a small apartment block. Luca said something about "prohibito" and a startled Chinese fellow shouted at me in Italian out of his apartment window. I'm not sure the resultant pic was worth all that effort but the thought was there. The hill is steep here, the next corner is the Grande Albergo Miramare, a gentle right-hander referring to another hotel that is no longer standing. More gaps in the scenery. "Bombed!"

At Belvedere, the next turn, we went right and up again and then parked up at Ponticello, the highest part of the circuit. You'll notice that, in some of the pictures, there's a checkerboard paint job on the concrete. Luca now blathered on a bit, I got the gist of it; there was an historic motorbike race here a few years ago and the place had a lick of paint. Luca is clearly frustrated at the lack of interest in the circuit by the local council; Ospedaletti really should be a tourist hotspot like Monaco he says. I agree.

We take some pictures then drive down the hill, Corsa Bellavistas, a left, and park up again on the corner of Corsa Guglielmo Marconi and Via de Medici. The 1947 clockwise version of this circuit came up here from the coast road below, but today, it's a 30 kph one-way street and no one in their right mind would take a racing car along it. Luca tries and fails to recall the English name for this corner, which then descends into a game of charades in the street with him enthusiastically miming away. I try to follow him; "Not white, no, the opposite, black, yes? OK, Black! What's that, a dinosaur? No. Jeremy Beadle? No. Aaah! Chicken! OK. What's that? What are you doing Luca? Put it away, someone will see us! Ah, a *male*

chicken. A cockerel! The black cockerel corner? Yes."
Phew.

We stick to the '48 track, Curva delle Mimrose, a short
straight with a beautiful view of the Med to the left, and
then a double apex to a downhill left-hander called
Quadrata. Remembering to give way, we join the SS1
coast road which is also the main straight, palm trees on
the right and the sea not far behind. Back to Piccadilly,
accidentally through a red light bang outside the police
station, a brief apology to a chap in a uniform fit for
pantomime, then another lap.

Ospedaletti is free from Monaco's congestion, no badly parked Ferraris or dithering tourists hampering the hoon; with the mostly unrestored buildings sat amongst the palm trees, you can imagine the thrill of screaming down the straight in a vintage Maserati, even if you're in a modern MINI. In 1948, the pack did 85 laps on skinny tyres and the fastest lap time over the 187 miles they raced was 61 mph, on a road surface best suited for livestock. Epic stuff. The result was a triumphant first win for Ascari and a 1-2-3 for Maserati.

I had little time left before needing to return the car and fly home but wanted another lap, just for fun, although it was now getting dark. Luca had been enjoying the ride and ignoring his permanently ringing phone. A VW Touran driver catches us up at the Belvedere corner, overtakes like only an Italian can and then stops dead in the middle of the road. A heavily pregnant woman is shouting like a machine gun at Luca. It's Mrs. Luca. As they have a domestic, my mind wanders off. The Ferrari and Maserati marques make the perfect analogy for Monaco and San Remo. Monaco is fun but overly fashionable, rather obvious and ostentatious. San Remo is stylish, fascinating and welcoming. Mrs. Luca eventually runs out of breath/bullets and then smiles. She's lovely. She was also due to give birth at any moment and had been worrying about Luca thundering around the streets with some random Englishman. Luca smiled. I smiled. They kindly invite me to dinner but I had to race for my plane. I wish I had a Maserati. I wish racing would grace these streets again.

Nürburgring in an Artega: the mother of all upgrades

Car;   Rented Artega GT. A what? An Artega GT.

Location;   The Nürburgring, Germanland.

Duration;   24 hours plus flights there and back.

It was supposed to be a safe way to enjoy some
Nürburgringery. Instead of slogging across Europe in my
own car, crossing my fingers that my insurer would help if
I had an off and risking life and limb on the Nordschleife, I
booked a cheap flight from Birmingham to Cologne,
rented a car to get me to the 'Ring, then picked up a car
from Rent4Ring and did the less risky Grand Prix circuit
instead. It should have been an MX-5, but I got the
mother of all upgrades. I got an Artega GT.

After signing some paperwork I daren't read, I hopped in
while Fredy (one 'd') gave me an introduction to the
Artega. It comes with a V6 sourced from a VW Passat R36,
a DSG gearbox and roughly 300 horses to propel it. In
addition to the VW drivetrain, most of the trim bits and
bobs are Wolfsburg-sourced too, although it has some
unique geeky features. The central console has an iPod-
style wheel for the wing mirrors and there's a flatscreen
displaying most of the cabin controls, operated by touch-
sensitive buttons. The dials are mostly LCD too, and
there's a neat party trick where you can flip and
customise the dials. In fact, the whole dash set-up is PC-
based and user-customisable. The window switches look
like old-school winders, but act like levers, with the round
grip styled like a tyre. Sounds gimmicky but I was
impressed. There is a useful space behind the seats and
plenty of elbow room. It looks and feels like a VW Evora. I

pretended to listen to the important details while inwardly screamed "let me drive!"

The Nürburgring Grand Prix circuit can be accessed for about 20 minutes at a time, tickets bought from a little shop to the right of the Dorint Hotel in the 'historic paddock' area. This is a lovely little square which has a feel of the hospitality of the circuit of old. Currywurst and chips, a decent beer and lots of interesting machinery parked up and friendly owners to talk to. None of the crush and hassle of a public session on the more popular Nordschleife. Buy your ticket, drive down the tunnel, in the pits and out on track with a handful of others. The same track that occasionally holds F1 even today. There's huge run-off and a mix of high- and low-speed corners to test you. Twenty minutes is enough in an easy-going MX-5. In the Artega GT, I was sweating after ten.

Excuse the stock picture by the way. I was too busy driving to take my own pictures this time. The GT sounds great. I appreciate that the industry is moving away from eights and sixes in favour of turbo'd fours, but there is no substitute for the aural pleasure of an engine like this. But it's not all good. I'm not a fan of the DSG box in any car, I don't care if it saves a split second to 60 mph, I prefer some stick-stirring involvement. After a few plays with it, I got bored and left it in drive. The electric power steering initially feels light but feels meatier on the move. The mirrors, viewed from the driving seat, are HUGE. You will lose people, cars and small buildings behind them. I guess this is an EU safety thing to do with the area of mirror glass, but it's a safety feature that is, simply, unsafe. Easily resolved though, I imagine. This particular car was fitted with Endless brake pads, which, although work very effectively, squeal like Justin Bieber on a night on D-wing. The car weighs just 100 kg more than an Evora but it seemed heavier, perhaps a psychological side effect of the Teutonic cabin. How does it handle? Well, beautifully, actually. On an early lap of the GP circuit, I got a bit lost, forgetting the second curve on the Schumacher 'S' and ending up on the wrong bit of tarmac, as my passenger shouted, "THE ANSWER'S IN THE NAME, IT'S NOT THE SCHUMACHER 'C', Y'BERK!" The handling was forgiving, thankfully, and I easily heaved the Artega in the right direction. The stats state 0–62 in 4.8 seconds and a top whack of around 170 mph, which felt right and it was utterly composed at high speed. Unlike me.

It's no secret I'm a Lotus fan, but at roughly £70k, you'd be daft not to consider the Artega as an alternative to an Evora S. The trim bits are more Lupo than Metro and it offers an equally exciting drive as the Lotus. I haven't driven a Cayman for a while, but a virtual 'head-to-head' in my er… head sees Stuttgart's work beaten by the Artega, particularly in the areas of styling and ride quality. Artega have relatively modest plans for expansion and we wish them the very best of luck. I wonder if they'll do a right-hand-drive one?

Session over, I charged about the local roads in the
Artega, savouring every minute I'd paid for. Locals and the
Polizei don't seem to mind enthusiastic driving as long as
you behave through the villages and don't act the loon.
The track is the place for that.

On the road out of Adenau, by chance, I spotted a yard
full of British Leyland cack. I had to investigate. It turned
out to be the business of a very tall, very German German
called Klinghammer, who is a BL specialist. From French-
registered Triumph 2000s to badly pranged Minis, he had
one of everything from the era when BL were at their
nadir. Yet, when we got chatting, he loved them. To him,
they had a charm and character missing from modern
cars. They were good designs, built badly, and his little
workshop put them right.

Customers came from far afield for his expertise. Many of the cars were his own, such as an SD1 and an Austin 1000. He was clearly mental. I liked him a lot. He locked up for the day, folded himself into his Metro Turbo (yes, red seat belts), said something about Hydragas and shot off up the hill.

I returned the Artega, only noticing then that the paperwork I signed had a €15,000 insurance excess in the event of an accident. Fifteen grand! So much for a risk-free trip to the 'Ring. The Artega GT was great, but renting an MX-5 makes more sense.

Footnote: Since writing this, I believe Artega went bust, were restarted and went bust a second time. I clearly know nothing about business.

Lotus vs. last orders

Car;   Loaned Lotus Elise Club Racer. Just as
                delicious bubble and squeak is made from
                leftovers, the Elise is Rover and Toyota
                scraps cooked up good and enough for a
                Michelin star.

Location;   From my local boozer in the East
                Midlands of England to Reims and back.

Duration;   12 and a half hours dead. Get the drinks
                in.

During the Dany Bahar era, Lotus chucked money at all
sorts of nonsense. They also chucked car keys at anyone
who asked them nicely. Even so, I did not expect them to
give me an Elise Club Racer when I asked and was so
surprised when they agreed that I hadn't even got a plan
of what I could do with it. So I went to the pub with my
old chum Dr. O. He calls himself the number one driver; I
call him talking ballast. I fancied a straightener before
getting on the beer but the landlord apologised for being
out of Champagne. An idea was born. Could we dash to
Reims to buy a bottle of bubbly and get back to the pub
before last orders that same day? We limboed into the
Lotus.

Leaving our pork scratchings untouched, we left Leicestershire sharpish, picking up passports and cameras from home, and fighting over the keys to the Elise. I shouted our booking over the phone to Eurotunnel as the Elise headed down the M1, pounded around the M25, arriving at Folkestone with barely enough time to apply beam deflectors and ponder the effectiveness of a magnetic GB sticker on plastic panels. The Club Racer is rather sparsely equipped; as standard, you have to make do with no stereo, no sound deadening and no passenger footrest. The roof is an optional extra. There is simply no excess fat on its aluminium frame; even the battery and badges are lighter than usual. It saves 24 kg over standard and (not that we're usually bothered but…) does a combined 45 mpg. The suspension and exhaust are fettled for optimum performance and it grips like a cat up a curtain. Dr. O, when not being the number one driver, was subconsciously making 'braaap, braaaaaap, bop-bop-bop, braaaaaaaaap' noises. The Elise makes you feel like a kid. It's a great feeling. Driving an Elise at high speeds is noisy but not uncomfortable. In order to make it back in time, we had to maintain a high average speed. This meant driving bang on the speed limit everywhere. Doing so, you obsess about the lost seconds when braking and accelerating. Fortunately, like all Lotus cars, the Elise seemingly has no heft and does the going and stopping stuff without a nanosecond's hesitation.

We whizzed down to Kent, Eurotunnelled, then flat out across northern France on the A26 autoroute in our booze-cruise missile. UK plates make the car invisible to fixed cameras and my talking ballast was watching for gendarmes. He spotted one speed trap, just outside Arras. They had an ancient, dark blue Peugeot 306 parked in the shade, half behind the concrete pillar of a bridge over the autoroute. In this crappy old car was a policeman with a radar gun and a radio. If you're much over the 130 kph limit (my guess is <=10% over this and you're probably in the clear), then he radios his colleagues, who are waiting maybe 5–10 km up the road, to flag you down and beast you. We slowed as we passed them, then stuck a few % on what we thought we could get away with to make up for this temporary slowing of pace.

Pommery was our destination, one of Reims' biggest Champagne houses with the original cellars (called crayères) created by Romans during their occupation of Gaul. We could have chosen another Champagne house but I liked the fact that founder, Louise Pommery, built a Tudor Elizabethan mansion in Reims in a nod to her most loyal customers, the British. She was also the first to make a 'brut' Champagne, with no added sugar, and was one of the first employers in France to create a retirement and health fund for her employees.

The Elise hopped over the cobbles. We parked directly outside, bought a brace of Jeroboams and took a few snaps whilst trying to fend off a swarm of excited children. An uninvited security guard stood with the car and, I'm quite sure, imagined that it was his. Outside the cathedral, everyone from kids on bikes to passing pensioners stopped to admire the Elise. Grown men pretended not to look overly interested whilst taking sneaky snaps with their iPhones. Everyone smiles at an Elise. Even one in 'Scottish Nude' blue.

Just outside Reims and roughly on our route is a place called Gueux (pronounced 'goo'), which staged F1 races from 1950 to 1966. The circuit is essentially a triangle on public roads and races here were famed for their high speeds. On the start–finish straight, the faded grandstands, pits and other decaying buildings are still present. There is an incredible atmosphere here. There are no shops or tourist information, and you're left to ignore the 'KEEP OFF' signs and explore an historic site, including the control tower with a cold wind blowing through its glassless windows. Crumbling facades advertise long-gone brands.

We took a few pics as the weather reminded us it was January and the light started to fade. The last F1 race at Reims saw the three Lotus entrants all score DNFs, with clutch, oil leak and gearbox failures. Ours felt taut and tireless. After a quick hit of coffee and a squashed pain au chocolat, we headed back to Calais for the return crossing. Our race against "time gentlemen, please" was on.

On leaving Gueux, Dr. O, the useless cretin, managed to send us west instead of north and we were so on it that we didn't notice until we nearly hit Paris. A quick re-calculation and we cut cross-country. The 1.6 litre engine has just 134 bhp and needs full use of the six gears to wind it up to speed, but is capable of comfortably hacking through the hills at great pace. Porsche fans might snort at the comparative lack of gadgets, modest horsepower and the 'let's go camping' technology employed in the roof. They'd be missing the point of Hethel's car entirely though. Everything in the Elise is done to inform and reward the driver in a refreshingly straightforward way. No technology to flatter ham-footed drivers, no acronyms to impress pub bores, no autobahn-only performance stats. Less is more. The Elise zig-zagged cross-country and thanks to that magically 'instant' go and stop ability, we still maintained a decent lick.

We finally picked up the right autoroute. Some man maths set our new cruising speed, balancing the few scant hours we had left against the briskest pace we could make without attracting the long arm of the lurking gendarmes. We *just* made the Eurotunnel on time, chatted to the inevitable friendly crowd that gathered and hit Kent late with a 3-hour drive back to Leicestershire to catch last orders. The south-east of England was busy with blinkered commuters and the M25 looked ugly. So we went up the M11 and cross-country via the A14, A6 and one of my favourite roads, the B6047. The Elise had been more than happy on highways, but where we expected it to come alive was on potholed, bendy B-roads. The B6047 was our home straight, but it's far from straight. Despite the darkness, damp tarmac and dimly lit tractors, the Elise tore through hilly countryside with ease. You brake later, there is complete steering feel and you can elbow it into apexes with great accuracy. Road surface imperfections are transmitted without tormenting.

There is insufficient space in this chapter for me to explain how good the Elise drives at speed in these conditions. I urge you to try one. We weren't tired and Dr. O was still making 'braaap' noises as we crossed the border into Leicestershire and simply nailed it home. We had to. I'm not detailing the final leg—it runs past my house, to my local. We parked it like a drunk driver and dashed in at 10.50 pm. Champagne anyone?

The landlord had to be shown the Eurotunnel ticket and receipt from the Champagne house before he believed how far we'd gone in such a short time. We could have taken something German on this jaunt instead, but anything other than a Lotus would have felt like a bus trip to the off-licence, and tasted like Liebfraumilch.

In 2012, Bahar lost his job amid allegations that he was misusing company funds for extravagant expenses. It seems he put £1.2 million on expenses, including helicopter travel, watches and decorating two houses. He sued for £6.7 million. Lotus sued him back for £2.5 million. I got lost in the legal wrangle after that, but Bahar buggered off to Dubai and Lotus are (thankfully) still in business. But I miss the crazy days when they'd give press car keys to the likes of me without question.

Sickday roadtrippers

Car;   My own BMW E46 330Ci. No, I couldn't
                  afford an M3.

Location;   The evo Triangle, Wales.

Duration;   If you're off work sick for seven days or
                  fewer, your employer should not ask for a
                  sick note.

Monday afternoon; start to use the 'poorly voice' in the
office. Tuesday morning; call in sick. Tuesday midday;
meet other sickday roadtrippers at the evo Triangle. It's a
bit of a drag up the A5 into Wales, but I can see why evo
and other mags use this area for road tests: it has a little
bit of everything and is the perfect place to spend a day
with the phone set to divert. I took my own E46 330Ci and
met a 350Z GT, a 986 Boxster S and an R32 Skyline. We
had a straight six, a V6, a flat 6 and a turbo'd six. This
chapter could have been called 'the joy of six', but I
digress. We met, gave each other's wheels an
appreciative nod and set off. I had intended to take it
easy. This time, it was my car and in a country which
could quite easily put points on my licence, or worse,
should I get it really wrong.

The Skyline was hard to follow; it was thrown into corners
with the confidence of 4WD, had 400 bhp on tap on the
straights and spewed fuel and flames on whoever was
behind it. I saw it roast a stray sheep. A triangle is a pretty
easy shape to follow: left, left again and left again back to
the start, but that didn't stop the 350Z pilot getting lost
for a while. The Boxster S flowed beautifully through the
bends. The (probably unfounded) fear of big bills always
puts me off these, but there's no arguing with the driving

dynamics. It went like stink and sounded fantastic too. The 350Z I knew well having previously lumped it around Spa. The GT spec has great brakes, a torquey engine and the feeling nothing will break even if you are 15-point turning it round a Welsh farm track because you mistook a triangle for a dodecahedron. The 330CiS has that zingy BMW engine and decent steering feel, but standard brakes wilt under hard use and you feel the weight when heaving it off the line. No, I couldn't afford an M3. Quirks aside though, none of these cars would make a bad choice for a quick daily driver capable of the odd trackday, run on a modest budget.

The Llyn Brenig (sod off spellchecker, I *meant* to type that) nature reserve was an unlikely rendezvous for lunch, any wildlife having been either scared off by 24 cylinders or burned alive by the fiery Skyline which had, incidentally, just been repaired after an off at the 'Ring and was struggling for grip on track-biased rubber.

Boxster boy conformed to stereotyping by double parking then spending lunch fretting over people gobbing on his car. I was probably mistaken for a sales reptile in the (comparatively) understated BMW, the subtle //M Sport badges having been mostly nicked by local Barries looking for a visual upgrade, the gits. Still, it's about how they drive, not how they look, right? There are plenty of tasty bits on the Triangle. The high-speed flowing straights of the A543 side were my fave, giving kippered brakes a little time to cool, and the tarmac is fresh and grippy. Nice. You know how evo magazine's action shots always seem to picture the featured car airborne? There's a nice yump near the turning for Pentre-Llyn-Cymmer (what that's worth at Scrabble?) where you can recreate that if you're so inclined. You do need to behave yourself though: scamera signs (and, therefore, vans) are common here, and it's annoying enough stomping on the brakes only to find that the white van on the horizon is actually a plumber stopped for a sarnie.

Welsh scenery is great, the roads are varied and challenging, and it's not that far away... So don't sit there, looking at the clock and wondering if Doreen from accounts has paid your expenses yet. Start using the 'poorly voice' now and treat yourself to a sickday road trip...

The Great Train Robbery

Car;   Press fleet-supplied long wheelbase
                        Jaguar XJR SuperSport.

Location;   Great Central Railway, Leicestershire.

Duration;   One day on the road, a life on the run.

I don't really do conventional car reviews. Frankly, I can't
be arsed. Rehashing press releases, rushing out stories
about the latest revision of trim, writing anodyne copy to
appease advertisers and not being too controversial for
fear of upsetting those who gave you the car to review. I
can't do that and, even if I could, who would buy a car on
my say-so? OK, so there *are* some great writers who find a
unique perspective and give an insight that others can't,
but I forget their names now. I gave up my subscriptions
to most car mags a long time ago. Is there a car that
doesn't get at least four out of five stars from evo's
reviewers for example? When I asked Jaguar for a car
(they had never heard of me, unsurprisingly), I was
surprised they even answered, let alone asked me where I
would like it delivering. I am more interested in the
history, the engineering, the motorsport pedigree and
general heritage of a marque than how many airbags it
has. It's about the people, not the product, not brown-
nosing Browns Lane. Maybe Jaguar's press lady was sick
of sycophancy too, because she sent me a lovely long
wheelbase XJR to relive a fascinating and largely forgotten
chapter of the infamous Great Train Robbery. The story of
'The Weasel'.

I don't believe that Roy 'The Weasel' James (above, centre) wanted to be a crook. Like other amateur racers of his time, he struggled to afford the latest chassis and engines needed to be successful in the lower formulae of British circuit racing. He did well in Formula Junior and moved into Formula Two, beating the likes of Mike Hailwood and was favourably compared to Jackie Stewart—but sponsorship eluded him. As his career reached the level where he could not rely on sheer talent alone to win, when he needed the best machinery to find that extra few percent needed to beat his contemporaries, something changed in him. Winners, particularly in motorsport, often seem to have an unpleasant edge. From Senna shunting Prost to quite a bit of what Schumacher did, winners have what seems like an unsporting nature needed to gain that extra little something which makes the top step of the podium much closer. Not even the police know exactly the timeframes of transition as Roy went from being a racing driver to being a racing driver who was a robber, to a robber who used to be a racing driver. We know when he died though. It was 1997, after some experimental surgery following a long prison sentence for wounding his father-in-law. He was, by then, a proper wrong 'un. He was also a lifelong Jag man.

Lazy journos will talk about cops and robbers, the Big Smoke and Jags being the getaway driver's car of choice, often without bothering to elaborate. But like all clichés, there is some truth in this. Roy James liked the performance, the handling and the space for loot. There are anecdotal stories from when his money ran out and he was desperate to go racing, that he robbed John Cooper of his silverware and melted it down. Of driving his Jaguar Mark 2 down to Monaco to burgle a hotel. As the police upgraded their Jaguars, he upgraded his—by burgling the competition department of Jaguar's own Le Mans team.

His reputation reached the paddock. There's a story of him being awarded a cup at Cadwell (I think) and the commentator announcing over the tannoy, "That's the last anyone will see of *that*". His nickname came not from his personality but from his appearance; lithe, flexible and strong. He didn't drink much and ate carefully, something second nature to today's racers but it marked him out, back then, as being that little bit better prepared than everyone else. He even practiced jumping off roofs near his North London home to escape, piling up rubbish to deter followers, but leaving a tiny patch for him to land safely, with turf lifted to help soften the landing.

Roy came to the attention of Bruce Reynolds (mastermind of the Great Train Robbery) and was offered the job as getaway driver in a daring heist on an airline. The gang dressed as city gents, with briefcases and bowler hats, and sat in the departures hall of Heathrow Airport. When the airline's wages van arrived, they clobbered the staff and made their escape. Roy was driving. He rammed another car, went through red lights and had his brake lights wired so he could operate them by a switch, preventing pursuers from detecting his braking points. Despite hot pursuit from Jaguar-driving policemen, he made good their escape. By now, the police knew who he was—who else could evade them so easily as a professional racing driver with criminal contacts? He took his share of the cash to Brabham, emptied the lot on the desk and ordered a new BT6 single-seater.

Fans of historic racing will know that Brabham was later run by Bernie Ecclestone. We'll come back to him. Roy was successful in this BT6 but the police were on to him, nearly catching him at Goodwood before he scarpered, having been tipped off. By now, perhaps buoyed by his success, the balance had shifted from him being a racer to a robber. The Great Train Robbery was planned and Roy was a bit-part player in it, driving the army Land Rover needed to shift the sacks of cash; £2.6 million of it, about £50 million in today's money. The gang left a fingerprint on a Monopoly 'get out of jail' card and the rest is history. Roy had bought a new E-Type with his share of the money but was finally caught later in 1963.

I took the Jaguar to the Great Central Railway in Leicestershire, met a mate with an S-Type (no, not *that* S-Type) and we compared the drive. The S-Type is essentially a Mark 2 with independent rear suspension, a set-up that was still used, identical parts and all, on other Jaguars and even Aston Martins up until quite recently. It is a great design. These cars have a wonderfully connected but simultaneously cosseting ride quality that rightly wins plaudits from the few writers who bother to put the reader in the driver's seat with their words. The cabin is narrow, the dash a bit creaky and even 3.4 litres don't propel it *that* quickly, but what charm, what character. The XJR is simply a monster. Too much power (540 bhp) for the rear tyres, a face like a kicked bulldog and boot space for enough small arms to start a civil war. Go and try one. You will want to start an insurrection.

We retold the story, posed besides rolling stock of the same vintage as the train robbery and mostly performed burnouts in the cindered yards amongst the locomotives, acting like hoodlums and loving it. Bernie's name came up again. After being released from his sentence, Roy was keen on a return to racing and Bernie encouraged someone to give him a chance. He broke his leg in practice and ended up smuggling, dealing and God knows what else. Bernie gave him a job. Perhaps mindful of Roy's skills in melting down stolen trophies, he employed him to make the F1 constructors' trophy. Why be so kind to an outcast? This relationship probably contributed to the rumour that Bernie himself was involved in the Great Train Robbery but, when interviewed, he once said "there wasn't enough money on the train for me to bother robbing it". He's a loveable rogue, Bernie, and so was Roy.

I'm surprised that no one has made a film about Roy's life. There are many more tales scattered around that need pulling together and scripting. My stab at it can be found on YouTube somewhere. If there's a filmmaker reading this, I'd like to volunteer for the lead role of a blockbuster. My driving, robbing and legging it skills are a bit rubbish compared to Roy, but we can CGI all that, can't we? Let's do a modern remake, with an XJR. Is it any good? It must be. It got at least 4 stars in evo.

Fear and loathing in Las Vegas

Car;	Rented Ford Mustang Convertible, 2.3 litre V6. Made sense over there, if not anywhere else.
Location;	Houston, Los Angeles, the arse end of Nevada and Las Vegas, USA.
Duration;	I was too mashed to remember. A week, ish?

Road trips need a reason. I had been engrossed in the motoring records of a hundred years ago, tales of Scott of the Antarctic taking an Austin on the ice, for example. Fastest, highest, coldest, furthest—it seemed like so many things had been conquered barely a hundred years after the car had been invented. What was left for a man of modest means, like me? Instead of looking outwards, at physical challenges, I had started looking inwards, at psychological ones. One of my favourite road trip stories didn't involve any great distance or speed, as such, but (and I apologise if this sounds rather wanky), a journey into the mind. "Fear and Loathing in Las Vegas" is a novel about a quest to understand the American dream. That is something that seems, to me, tied up in material things; success, money, cars. I wanted a taste of that, not expecting any eureka moment (what Englishman could ever truly understand the American psyche anyway; they don't even play cricket for goodness sake) but perhaps an enlightening glimpse of what the American dream means. I booked a flight and packed a copy of "Fear and Loathing in Las Vegas" to re-read on the long journey over the Atlantic.

The cab collected me for the trip to London Heathrow and my driver was Warren, an old friend I last saw nearly 20 years ago, a pleasant surprise. I told him what I was up to. He hadn't read the book. He hadn't even heard of it. He told me about spending time with family in the Caribbean and eating fresh mango in the sunshine, and we laughed about putting gravel down Clive Evans' underpants at school. Clive is now a second-hand car salesman.

The M1 was hell. The M25 was hell. The Norwegian was waiting for me at Terminal 5 and we checked in, did the passport thing and stuffed ourselves aboard the American Airlines flight to Houston. Plastic-bagged blankets and crap coffee. The Norwegian hadn't read the book either but pretended to listen as I tried to explain cultural revolution, the quest for the American dream and the joy of a meandering road trip. He brightened up at the bit about sex, drugs and rock and roll. "This meal isn't very big", he said. It looked like microwaved rabbit foetus served with Pritt Stick cheese and crackers. Our air hostess was English and she poured the coffee under the watchful eye of a senior colleague; "You don't want to drink this", she whispered. She was right.

George Bush Intercontinental Airport offered queues, potato-shaped people in polyester uniforms telling you where to stand and a rental car so bland that I didn't even take a picture. Hotel. Sleep. Wake up at 3 am. Later, we walked to the Waffle House. I just wanted some porridge, orange juice made from an orange and a cup of tea with semi-skimmed milk and half a sugar because I am English.

A woman in a smock stretched over her space-hopper figure looked really offended; "NO WAFFLES?!" Her bug eyes nearly popped out of her fat face. I had waffles with "city ham". No, I've no idea either. The Norwegian had the works. And my leftovers. "Small portions", he said. Who is paying for this? Not me or him. The protagonist of the book (if you haven't read it yet, you should—it's loads better than this one) is a journalist who gets an advance for reporting on a race in the desert. The protagonist of my book, me, got an advance for some consultancy in the oil and gas industry. Both of them piss it up the wall, eventually, in a rough-arsed quest for some sort of enlightenment. So, then—the pub. No aperitifs, just three or four pints of synthetic lager and a beautifully snarky barmaid. Someone put Green Day on the jukebox. She emptied her pot of tips into his hand and asked him to leave. She knew the beer was piss and gave us glasses of 'Bald Knob' whiskey. It tastes exactly like winky. I imagine. The Norwegian was thoroughly 'in drink' by now and had been cornered by a slightly-too-friendly chap with a DIY haircut and an iPad who wanted to show us pictures of his Lamborghini, yet only had pictures of his dog's infected stitches. We left the peanuts. The Norwegian mentioned the American dream and was given precise instructions of where we could go to shoot a gun. And see alligators. Sadly, Mr. Dog-stitches didn't think it would be possible to combine the two. I'd had enough and the barmaid rescued us. "Try this place", she said, and wrote down a list of other places to try: Catbirds, Royal Oak, The Anvil. Maybe she'd had enough of us.

A cab came. Patrick was the driver; strong Nigerian accent and loud radio in his Toyota minivan. The booze, humidity and tiredness were catching up on me and the country music was like a mosquito in my head. The Norwegian complained, "You don't really like this rubbish, do you Patrick? Whatever you listen to at home—play that please". We got Fela Kuti. Patrick beamed and he translated some of the lyrics. One I'd heard before, "Water, him no get enemy", followed by one of Patrick's favourites, "Woman! I'm going to beat you like you've been in an accident!" He laughed and repeated it in case we missed it. We tipped heavily and got out quick at Catbirds. A trendy place.

I am not a trendy person. The last time I tried trendy facial hair, I looked like I'd glued pubes to my face. Not even my own pubes. A restorative G&T worked wonders for my mood. The trendy people in Catbirds were nice. We drank 'Blonde Bombshell' from cans and listened to a DJ play Édith Piaf. The Norwegian was convinced they were smaller than average cans and drank twice as many as me. We decided to walk back to the hotel, past a tattoo parlour and a creepy clapboard house with a fortune teller's sign outside and an orange Dodge Charger round the back. There were homeless people with their world in a shopping trolley. I didn't want to ask them about the American dream in case they thought I was being a smart-arse. No bar at the hotel. No minibar in the room. No nightcap. We checked out of the hotel the following morning. Houston is horrible. On a back road to the airport, there was a large run-down shop selling cowboy stuff and the Norwegian, a bit brittle from the night before, decided that the American dream might be something you wear.

The shop was large, stocked with every bit of yee-ha attire you can imagine. A hands-on fifty-something female shop assistant (Cowgirl? Cow-woman? Cow-cougar?) showed us around. Saddles, shirts, jeans, boots, spurs and lots and lots of hats. The Norwegian tried on most of the hats and insisted on me appraising every single one for style, fit and "American dream-ness", before buying one. I think he already has a gun at home. And then off to the airport in our economy saloon car, Norwegian in his hat, me in the only pair of jeans I own, looking like a pair of slighty sore rejects from the Brokeback Mountain casting couch.

Houston to LAX Airport. Two hours lost (gained?) and humidity. For not very much money, Hertz will rent you a

Mustang. Mine was a white cabriolet, a V6 engine mated to an automatic gearbox that sounded (I imagine) like the cow-cougar woman having an oversquare poo.

Exiting the airport, we got a bit disorientated and drove through a suburb called Compton, which I recalled from the NWA track "Straight Outta [sic] Compton", which includes the lyrics "crazy mother*****r named Ice Cube". I put the roof up. Happily, we never got to meet Mr. Cube or any of his ilk and went up the coast and listened to someone talk about their wonky oil rig instead. Then to an English pub for bottled Budweiser with tequila chasers beneath a Greek flag hung upside down and a massive screen showing baseball, *just* like we do in England.

Baseball; what a pointless sport. It seems like a kind of cricket with the aim of running around in the dirt back to where you started, played by portly Hispanics in pyjamas. I asked the barman what makes this an English pub and, after about three minutes of gob-open thinking, he pointed at a dartboard in the corner. Time to go. Where do we find the American dream around here? There were two suggestions from boozing locals, the first being to visit a winery, which the Norwegian (being a connoisseur of all things alcoholic) sniffed at. Wrong kind of *terroir*, apparently. The second suggestion was to take a budget flight to Vegas. We'd had quite enough budget flying thank you very much, and looked at a map. It didn't look far and we had a Mustang. An early night would be the sensible thing to do, so we sat drinking cocktails until the small hours and got what felt like 30 seconds sleep before throwing luggage into the boot, taking care not to crush the Norwegian's cowboy hat.

America is a big place. The less charming Americans tell you that England (the UK/London/Scotland/Great Britain/Yerp, it's all the same to them) will fit 12 times into their lunch box. That's probably right.

With the Norwegian at the helm, we bounded down the Pacific Coast Highway, a beautiful road, and, before turning inland, we stopped at a pretty beach, accessed by crossing a broken fence and a railway track. The Norwegian had a swim. I had a paddle. My shins were blistering in the heat. I called Dad to tell him I was standing in the Pacific. "The last Duisberg to visit the Pacific was there to shoot Japs", he said, before ringing off as he had to get to the tip before it closed. There's nothing like my dad to bring me back to Earth. My head was thumping. Hangover, dehydration and too much sun, probably. In the book, the characters deal with paranoia brought on by a cocktail of drugs. I'd had just cocktails and was suffering the exact same. Back in the car, through LA's suburban slums and then east towards Las Vegas. It didn't look far on the tatty map in the pub a few hours before. A Camaro was following us. Probably going the same way. We pulled off the highway and back on again.

He did the same. We wound the Mustang up a few mph. He did the same. It was now bloody hot, 42 degrees, but having paid for a cabriolet, we were not going to have the roof up unless absolutely necessary. We'd run out of cash and our last few cents went on a small bottle of water to share. The Norwegian was tetchy. He was struggling to understand my explanation of 'wash-back'. Also, his hat had got a bit squashed the night before. I suspect he had slept in it, but he thought I had sat on it. Either could be true. The black Camaro sat about 200 metres behind us. Single occupant. Policeman? My iPhone told us we still had four hours drive to Vegas before packing up as it had gotten too hot. The Camaro thankfully vanished.

We needed petrol and found what seemed like the only petrol station for miles. Pull up at the pumps, open the flap, click. Nothing. Card in the machine. Nothing. Inside the shop for help. The harridan behind the counter had the complexion of a five-pound note that's been through the wash twice. I'll spare you the full transcript of the very strained conversation, but it seems that you have to prepay a fixed amount for your petrol (back to the car for your passport as they don't accept cards without ID), fill your car to that amount or less, then back to the desk where fiver-face then credits your card if you've used less fuel than you've prepaid. This is complex enough without a hangover and the mind arguing with itself, but I have no idea of the cost of fuel in California in real money, nor how big the Mustang's tank is, and politely asking her for "fifty quid's worth please, love" did me no good whatsoever. The Norwegian had fallen asleep. I drank some of the water and poured the rest on his hat. My turn to drive.

This book isn't about car reviews. One man's Mustang is another man's donkey, but I ought to say a few words about it. As you'd expect, the V6 is slow and it changes direction gingerly, like John Prescott leaving a buffet table with a plate full of Scotch eggs in each hand. It has an electric roof, huge cup holders, an automatic box with manual override (that somehow makes it worse) and very good air conditioning. There's a menu on the dash offering 'track apps', where you can record 0–60 mph and 1/4 mile times. It's no iDrive. Middle America aspires to this car, so I'm told. The original Mustang was a symbol of freedom, something for the working man to show he'd made it and be proud. They're still great value for money today, but the message it gives in the USA is very different to that it would give in Britain. Actually, as a road trip motor, it makes perfect sense. Even if this road trip itself doesn't make much sense yet.

The anti-hero in the book drives increasingly erratically, playing with the risk of being stopped by the police, then playing with the policeman when he inevitably does get stopped—being obviously drunk and only slightly hiding it, seeing how far he can push the officer without getting a ticket. I have put many things on expenses in my time and gotten away with it (a flight in a private helicopter being perhaps my cheekiest), but I could not (and still cannot) afford to end up behind bars. So, cruise control on, decent tunes selected (Lalo Schifrin) and a hard blat across increasingly deserted landscape. The desert was like nothing I had seen before, barren and beautiful. Next stop in the blistering midday sun on the road to Vegas; Barstow.

Now, I've been to some arse-end of Nowhereville places, but Barstow is surely the arse-end of the arse-end of Nowhereville. A dust bowl location with a handful of diners serving various forms of spiced cholesterol. The Norwegian was now awake and suspiciously studying his sodden hat. We picked a diner and accidentally ordered hamburgers, burritos, fries, Cokes and ice creams from staff who spoke Spanish very quickly and confused us. The Norwegian wolfed the lot, and mine, and questioned the portion size. "This American dream thing", he said, "it's bollocks, isn't it?" Sometimes, foreigners use English in a way we Brits can't better. I was beginning to wonder what we were doing here, in the desert, so far from home.

Back on the highway, an arrow-straight road with huge vistas, we had the highway to ourselves and, with the cruise control set to HIGH, we ate up the Mojave Desert. The sheer desolation of this place is breathtaking. It was hotter than Hades. At an exit signposted Field Road, I pulled off for a luminescent wee. No field on Field Road. Just desert. And someone else who was looking for the American dream. If the 'PEACLUV' registration plate wasn't a giveaway, the marijuana leaf mural and Bob Marley flag was. Hippies.

A 1960s International Loadstar bus with a VW camper welded on top was home to a smelly fellow whose name I wrote on a bit of paper and subsequently lost. It wasn't his real name anyway. Let's call him Stench. He emerged from his broken down dream and politely laughed at two red-faced, heavily hungover Europeans suffering from sunstroke. He had some interesting tattoos, homemade clothing, facial piercings and tales of squatting in Rotterdam, Bristol and "that bit in between London and Scotland". He looked enviously at the Norwegian's hat.

As we talked, I gentled shuffled into an upwind position of my fragrant friend. Stench and his girlfriend were travelling across the States in their bus/home and had broken down. His belongings were strewn across the desert. There was a surfboard optimistically lashed to the back of the truck.

"This isn't the dream", said the Norwegian disconsolately. "It's our dream", said Stench and then, inevitably, asked us for some money. We couldn't tow him as we were heading in the opposite direction, so left with a toodle pip. You can get to things that are far away in a short time if you drive very fast, explained the Norwegian (he's an engineer), so we sat at three figures with the music set to shuffle. "Into the Valley" by Skids. We crossed the border into Nevada and a place called Primm, which seems to be a sort of mini-Vegas for those who found the journey this far too much and flop over the finishing line into Nevada to desperately gamble at the first place they find. I suspect Primm entices/entraps many sun-scorched travellers who stagger around the bleached streets looking for Caesar's Palace before the vultures empty their pockets. Roller coasters, concrete, parking lots. We didn't stop.

More highway, then suddenly the black Camaro came out of nowhere and went past us at massive speed, rocking the wobbly Mustang as it went past. I tucked in behind a minivan; it had a tail-lift on the back with a mobility scooter on it. We saw a few of these contraptions, the lift part bobbing up and down, threatening to tip the scooter off the back and into our path. We didn't stop. The music shuffled to 'Viva Las Vegas' and there it was, rising out of the desert like Blackpool on crack. "What are we doing here?", asked the Norwegian. I didn't know either.

Google found a hotel. The Polo Towers Suites, 3745 Las Vegas Boulevard South, Las Vegas, NV 89109. An ambitiously priced place on the Vegas strip with brainless staff, tiny rooms, beds as comfortable as bookcases and a fountain in reception. The decor might have been designed by a Blue Square Conference League (North) WAG. Ugly families in leisurewear clogged the corridors. The price went up three times when trying to check-in.

We were knackered and they knew it. The Mustang was abandoned in someone's basement nearby. Google found us The Polo Towers Suites, 3745 Las Vegas Boulevard South, Las Vegas, NV 89109 and I hope Google now finds our two-word review of The Polo Towers Suites, 3745 Las Vegas Boulevard South, Las Vegas, NV 89109: "It's horrible."

We staggered onto the strip, eyes tired and gritty, lights everywhere. Oriental men tried to foist lap-dancing club flyers into your hand at every step. They were everywhere. They slapped their flyers in their palms like a nervous tic, then lunged forward aiming it at your hands, hoping your impulse is to take it from them. I have never had a greater urge to punch someone in my entire life. The only thing stopping me was the thought that there were thousands of the little bastards and they might retaliate en masse.

A bar. A very expensive Budweiser served by a barman who didn't like eye contact. Another beer. "It's gambling", said the Norwegian, "that's the point of this place, that's the dream" and we ambled into Caesar's Palace. Elvis wasn't in. I was disappointed. I wasn't sure what to expect; I'd only been to two casinos in my life: once in Monaco and another time in Leicester on a night out with an undercover detective who was watching bent Cypriot chippy owners launder ill-gotten gains. There are innocuous ATMs with a tiny sign explaining their hefty withdrawal fees. The Norwegian finally found a bank card that the ATM liked, got some cash and sat at a roulette table. He put everything on red. Spin. Black. Game over. "That wasn't fun", he said. The people were a mish-mash of middle America, stag dos, wedding parties, employees on a night out and a retired couple, him holding his hands out as she carefully counted their chips into them. The place smelled like a Scout hut. Men in those ghastly 3/4-length baggy shorts with socks and white trainers whooped, sobbed and argued with friends, wives and fiancées.

A fire alarm went off. The people feeding slot machines never even flinched. Another beer and a show. A woman danced woodenly to some RnB number and was joined by a pensioner in a staged act of random happiness. I drank warm Budweiser from a bottle. Then a bar, overlooking the strip, for margaritas that the Norwegian didn't rate. There were tattooed hookers with all the sex appeal of Jimmy Savile and a view of traffic, lights and a massive video display threatening a live show by Celine Dion. More casinos; the Flamingo, the Tropicana, the Bellagio, Luxor—all with the same rancid atmosphere, invasive lights, bad carpets and swarms of loud people racing to their ruin.

Rotund pensioners in mobility scooters sat at one-armed bandits, hen nights queuing in obviously uncomfortable shoes outside nightclubs and locals touting tat. There's a model of the Statue of Liberty, a model of the Eiffel Tower (minus the dog muck), fountains and light shows, and an endless throng of middle Americans burning money in the desperate hope of fleeting happiness. Another drink might make it palatable. More beer. A smashed woman overheard my accent; she was here from Basildon to get married. "Briwyunt, innit?", she shrieked through bad teeth as her bloke made a combined effort to hold her up and grope her at the same time. This is my idea of hell. Time to run.

We checked out of the "It's horrible" Polo Towers Suites, 3745 Las Vegas Boulevard South, Las Vegas, NV 89109. No hair of the dog. No breakfast. Another needlessly complicated gas station transaction. To drink; plenty of water and some coffee in huge disposable cups; no spoons for stirring, just useless thin plastic sticks. To eat; a large bag of those twisty doughnuts, chocolate and some yellow sweets that tasted like 9V battery terminals. We had both slept in and, in order to get back to LA for the return flight, we'd need to press on. Vegas dropped away from view in the mirror, and we ate, drank, made phone calls, discussed tunes and generally had a high-speed mobile picnic.

There was no sign of Stench when we passed his turn, but we pulled off the highway and drove on the old Route 66 that runs parallel to the new highway. Like plants growing near an oasis, there were a few signs of life near the highway exit, but the further away you got, the more scarce life became. Broken houses, gas stations with no pumps and a forecourt of broken glass, mobile homes with the walls kicked in. More desert. The artery of passing trade dried up. No soft edges anywhere, scratchy plants reclaiming their place, concrete, dust and silent despair. I parked the Mustang in the carport of a deserted house. Who had lived here? Why would anyone ever choose to live here where nature offers nothing to nourish life? As I stepped backwards to get a better photograph, the bushes scratched my legs and I nearly fell over the iron railings of a small grave. The headstone was a lump of rock, four screw holes where a plaque once was. All this talk of the American dream: it's nonsense, it makes a mockery of the poor buggers who clung to life with their fingernails here. Nuked by the sun. My face was peeling off and my tongue felt like underlay.

We drove on to another unpleasant surprise; where the old road rejoins the main highway stood two cops with radar gear. They were aiming at the highway and we'd unexpectedly approached from the old road instead. Lucky for us.

You can't really hear your own accent can you? (I say glass, not glarse). And yet, when faced with a bull-framed copper with a radar gun in one hand and a real gun in the other, I forgot my East Midlands roots and spoke like Terry-Thomas doing an impression of Prince Charles. I could barely understand the words that left my own lips but think I said hello. "What's the speed limit here?!", bellowed the policeman. I lied a reply. Convincingly, as it turned out. "Well it ain't a hundren ten!" We'd only been 'pootling along' I said. We hadn't noticed the police helicopter overhead; they'd spotted us long before we got here and were waiting. "I'm so dreadfully sorry", a phrase I have never used before in my life. A polite bollocking later, we were on our way. Cruise set to 100 mph, our logic being that we'd encountered one speed trap, so the chances of hitting another so soon would be pretty slim, and we headed west, fast, back to LA for the flight home.

A final meal at a quiet truck stop. I ordered the 'Good karma burger', purely on the strength of the name. The Norwegian ordered one of the dozens of variations of beefburger with fries. Sick of stale Bud, we ordered Dos

Equis beer XX, brewed to celebrate the turn of the millennium. The passing of time, the changing of a number, is that really something to celebrate? You may as well call it Tuesday. What's the point? I was jaded and cynical. It was acceptable beer, although my burger seemed a bit off. We tipped and, as I left, the waitress looked in my direction and said quietly to the sweaty chef, "Him, *he* ordered the vegetarian burger". And then the drive back to LA.

The Norwegian was exhausted and confused. We arrived at the airport, stopping to refuel the car. A homeless guy handled the pump. "I pump for tips", he explained, as I dug in my pocket for some change. The Norwegian misheard and corrected him, self-righteously, "Tits? We are not tits—we are *Europeans!*" I needed another drink.

And the American dream? The book drew no firm conclusion, ending in drug-fuelled chaos, but I think we'd had a glimpse of it in Vegas. Perhaps it's just an excuse to burn like a firework in the name of self-gratification, not caring that you're nothing but a smoking cardboard tube on the floor seconds later, not even thinking that far ahead. Spend, drink and shout. As the Norwegian succinctly said, "It's bollocks". It was a damn good excuse for a road trip though.

Winning a Renault Zoe

Car;   A Renault Zoe. Can I get a rewind?

Location;   No more than a 35-mile radius from
                home.

Duration;   Too long.

"Congratulations", said the email. "You've won a week with a Renault Zoe". I had entered a competition and first prize was a week with a blobby hatchback. Second prize was a month. *Ba-dum-tish!* The last (and only) Renault I'd had before caught fire with my kids in it. I hadn't been much of a fan since then and had my suspicions that their build quality and customer care hadn't improved in the mean time. Anyway, after writing a total pack of lies about how much I loved electric vehicles, I had a car for a week, but it soon went a bit Craig David. Sing along if you know the words.

I met this girl on Monday. She was delivered by a pimp/delivery man from Renault who explained all her controls and reassured me she is cheap and easy and wouldn't break down in a puddle of her own fluids because she's 100% electric.

I took her for a drink on Tuesday. The range dropped quicker than Craig David dropping knickers. The charging point in town was kaput and there wasn't another for miles. I minced her home with all the electricals off, just in case, and wished I was in the vintage Morris going the other way, a car which had racked up nearly a century's service because it is simple and robust.

We were making love by Wednesday. We weren't making love by Wednesday. An electrical system error message meant I wasn't allowed to make love to her and I wasn't to drive her either. OK, it just said I wasn't allowed to drive her. A call to Renault's dedicated recovery department was quite telling, "is it an electric car or a *normal* car?" they asked, but couldn't tell me if she was safe to drive or not. I called the local Renault main dealer who were similarly clueless, "ah, you need to call the electric vehicle people!", whoever they might be. Prior to the breakdown, the air con was limp, she shuddered at speed and the doors shut with exactly the same kinda clunk as a wheelie bin lid. Bo selector!

And on Thursday and Friday and Saturday... she was still broken. I did some sums. You'd have to do mega mileage to save enough petrol money to recover the price of buying her. My best effort on one charge had been a distance of about 70 miles (meaning a return journey radius of 35 miles). And then I have to plan routes that pass a charging point and hope it is working and available

(I inadvertently 'socket blocked' EV evangelist Robert 'Kryten' Llewellyn in a Tesla at the services). There are various membership fees to use the chargers, which are operated by many different companies. Electricity isn't free. Then there's the cost of installing a charger at home (with a SIM card in it so the government can monitor usage) and her battery must be leased at £70–£113 a month. All this adds up to too much. Oh, and she's a pretty joyless thing to drive. Can I get a rewind?*

We chilled on Sunday. She went back to Renault on a flatbed. The local Renault garage called and asked me to rate the repair they alleged she'd had. I explained that the car had gone back to Renault HQ still broken and that the car they claimed to have repaired had been sat on my driveway all week. I later heard that of the eight cars delivered that week, two had problems. Mine and another that kept fritzing its charger at home. The Renault Zoe is a frumpy, expensive and complex car sold and supported by a confused company. Renault sometimes makes great things, mostly called 'Cup', but I haven't got the time or patience for them to sort out Zoe's issues when there are many cheaper and more reliable options available. Renault gave me an iPad as a gift, perhaps hoping I'd never mention this episode. But, like Craig David says, *I'm not a man to play around baby. Ooh yeah.*

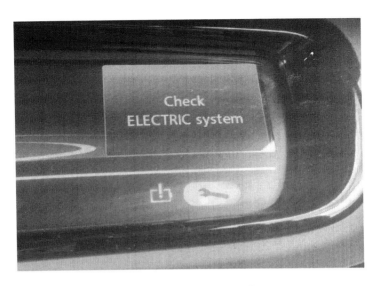

*A joke for both Craig David fans *and* electric motor engineers. You don't get this in What Car?

Wrecking a Rent-A-Wreck

Car;	Rented Ford Focus estate, 1.6 litre petrol. Damaged outside, diseased inside.
Location;	Oslo, north and keep heading north.
Duration;	A week.

Rent-A-Wreck is an American car rental company with a few franchises in Europe. In Norway, new cars are cripplingly expensive and it follows that car hire is cripplingly expensive. Rent-A-Wreck has a couple of locations there where cheapskate travellers, like me, can save a few kroner and rent a 10-year-old Ford Focus from them. I have had a Toyota Avensis from them before, and a Hyundai thingy, but the worst (in mechanical terms) and, therefore, the best (in entertainment terms) was a Ford Focus estate. Before I get into the sights, sounds and decaying smells of this machine, a bit of background as to how I came to be standing knee-deep in snow contemplating driving this heap up towards the Arctic Circle.

I had worked in Norway a lot and was fortunate to have the use of a skiing cabin in a very remote corner of the country, which belonged to a customer. I enjoy flailing about in the snow, pretending to be Roger Moore in "The Spy Who Loved Me". On this trip, I decided to take my reluctant (now ex) wife, our three daughters and one of their friends, along with another family. My wife lost her passport on the way to Stansted Airport, so missed the flight. My daughters' friend suffered from horrendous travel sickness and spewed heavily all over the inside of my own car. Then the motorway was closed and we nearly missed the Ryanair flight to what they optimistically called Oslo. So we arrived covered in vomit and stressed and collected the keys (from a frozen post box cable-tied to a fence round the back of the airport) to an ancient Ford Focus. My mate (also called Rich) had one the same. We rammed the kids, skis and luggage in them and set off in the heavy snow.

Winter tyres are compulsory in Norway. These are tyres much like the all-season ones most people use in the UK (and warmer places) but with a groovier pattern and a smidgen more grip. The locals use studded tyres, which give loads of grip and can be quickly mastered. Rent-A-Wreck cars came with the regular winter tyres, the type that Petter Solberg would struggle with on these roads. Fresh snow itself isn't particularly tricky to drive on. When it becomes compacted, it gets slipperier, and when it melts and then sets as ice, even more so. Take that and add compacted snow on top and it's the most viscous surface known to mankind. Yes, you know an accident is coming, but let me set the scene first.

Setting off on a very long journey, on unlit mountain roads, in near darkness, was foolhardy. And these wrecks were stuffed to capacity. It was like attempting to use a pedalo to cross the Atlantic. In January. With U-boats stalking you. The sickly kid honked again. The wipers packed up. Then the heater gave up. As I'm juggling all this, I am fending off text messages from my (now ex) wife, back in England, who is asking inane questions about where she might have left her passport. Then the engine management light came on. Some of the children cry, but perk up when they see that the Norwegian word for speed bump is '*fartdamper*'. Sickly kid honks again and says she wants to go home. My wife texts to apologise for losing her passport, then asks if her passport is perhaps in my pocket. It is not. The radio packs up. I stop to fit the snow chains in the boot.

The snow chains are in a plastic box. The last renter had put them back wet, and the box had frozen shut because the car was so cold because the heater didn't work. I opened the bonnet (which miraculously fixed the radio) and placed the box on the engine to thaw it out, so I could open it. After covering the engine in melted plastic box, I had some chains. Locals could probably fit a set in five minutes. It took me an hour. Then you drive with a weird thump-thump-thump sensation and, although your stopping distance improves, the car still understeers like a runaway ship. A text from the missus. "Is my passport in the drawer do you think?" My hands are too cold to type the swear words needed. I notice that the sickly kid's vomit has frozen in the footwell, which is nice because it stops the smell, although there is now a smell of burned plastic box coming from the engine bay. The road was climbing, it was getting colder and more remote, we were in a gorge alongside a river deep in the darkness below us, with rockface on one side and a low barrier on the other. The smell of sick came back. I felt sick too.

You'll know that an accident is coming. I knew an accident was coming. It was impossible not to have an accident, but we couldn't stay where we were, in the middle of nowhere, in the dark, with no other idiots attempting to use the same tiny road as us. I'm quite proud that I caught my skid. In ice skating terms, I performed a waltz followed by a toe loop, with the car eventually facing the right way having not hit anything. I pretended that it was intentional. As I looked in the mirror, I saw the following car, driven by my mate Rich, pirouette perfectly and ram a metal barrier. All low-speed stuff, but enough to kick the Focus' face right in. I got out to help and promptly fell on my face. I have never known a surface so slippery. The car was mostly broken, but it started and drove and, after a very, very long journey, we made it to the ski lodge. We skied, we drank, we saw the Northern Lights. It was beautiful.

But that's not the end of this chapter. A day later, at the precise time I thought I could relax, I got a text. "I've found my passport! It was in Kettering! I'm on the next flight!" I had to drive down the mountain, on the same lethal road, and then back again, further buggering up my trip. The flight home was no less eventful when a drunken Polish labourer told my kids there was a bomb on the plane, and I had to insist that the captain (who bore a striking resemblance to a drunken Polish labourer himself) remove the man from the plane before take-off. My car, in the long-stay, stank of vomit and the battery was flat. I'd have gladly swapped it for whatever Rent-A-Wreck would have offered.

A three-wheeled built vs. bought showdown

Car;   Borrowed Morgan 3 Wheeler. Three is
                the magic number.

Location;   Curborough circuit, England.

Duration;   One day, and what a day.

You might not know the pop group called The New Christy
Minstrels, but I'll bet you've heard their God-awful
cowboy song. It goes: *"Three wheels on my wagon, and
I'm still rolling along"*. That tune was stuck in my head, in
my helmet, as I roared across the Midlands in a shiny
press-fleet Morgan 3 Wheeler I'd borrowed. My
destination was Curborough sprint circuit, which was to
be the venue for a six-wheeled duel, the culmination of
weeks of increasingly edgy banter between Deltapig's
pilot, Mark, and myself.

Mark was quite sure that his home-built Del Boy deathtrap would beat £35k of lovingly hand-crafted Morgan 3 Wheeler. An interesting twist is that Mark is a professional driver. I have a man to wield my spanners and the most strenuous thing I've done in the M3W (as it's known in Malvern) is refill my pipe. I hadn't told Morgan what I was up to. I had requested a car for a comparison and review against another three-wheeler. Which was true, I suppose.

I arrived in good time to find that Mark was already there. He had needed a Tranny to tow his massively modified Reliant to the venue, whereas I had arrived under my own steam to smiles and waves from everyone. I am yet to meet anyone who doesn't like the M3W. Apart from looking fantastic, especially in these Gulf colours, it is rather entertaining to drive. It has a thumping 115 bhp two-cylinder S&S V-Twin bike engine (that's a lovely 1 litre per pot), an MX-5 gearbox and a snug tub to sit in. Kerb weight is a trim 550 kg, 0–60 mph takes perhaps six seconds and it maxes out at 115 mph. What home-built hero could beat that?

The build of Deltapig was being covered elsewhere in a specialist magazine. It started life as a Reliant Robin and is now a very silly thing indeed. I was surprised to see it runs on ethanol, has a turbo and has all superfluous fixtures and fittings removed to get the weight down—including the floor. The gearbox (scavenged from someone's back yard) had only just been fitted and Mark started to bore me with some tedious waffle about fuel and timing, before disappearing inside his contraption to finish his fettling ahead of our duel. I had a cup of tea. Now, I'm no race engineer, but I could see that, even with funny fuel and forced induction, Mark would have to be one hell of a driver to get Deltapig to corner properly. One wheel at the front means it would have a Vauxhall's level of understeer.

The M3W, where I sat to observe Mark's feverish spannering, has two wheels up front. My only concern in the Mog was putting the power down. It started to rain a little. I looked at the moistening track. A nice long straight, followed by a right-hand hairpin, a little right-left-right chicane called Molehill, a long looping right called Fradley, then back down the straight. Mark's encyclopaedic knowledge of racing lines, apexes and braking points would be largely negated by Curborough's simple layout. How hard can it be?

Time for a warm-up lap. A few people had turned up, some exchanged money, all of them watched intently as I flicked off the safety toggle and pressed the starter button in the centre of the Mog's padded dash. The engine feels lumpy and has a narrow torque band, meaning it goes thrap-thrap-thrap-umph as you quickly hit the limiter, the whole cockpit vibrating, rear end smearing rubber all over the track. The steering is a bit odd. That'll be something to do with the narrow front tyres, but the gear change and brakes are pretty perfect for me. "All the gear and no idea" was Mark's last taunt, but in a West Midlands accent that I struggled to comprehend.

The Mog's initial turn-in is sharp, but as soon as you start to lean on the front tyres, you realise that the whole shebang has been set up for safety. Colossal understeer. Suddenly, the homemade suspension set-up of Mark's leading wheel looked quite clever. Whatever he was mumbling about camber and caster became clear as I ploughed round the Fradley right-hander and thrap-thrap-thrap-umph'd my way back to the pits. Some of the people watching started arguing about money. Mark went for a lap. Despite suspension chopped down to nothing, it was clear that Deltapig cornered like a pot-bellied pig, leaning over and lifting an inside wheel in the bends, trike becoming bike.

It was clear that we couldn't race side by side. The 2-1 vs. 1-2 wheel layout meant very different handling characteristics and, therefore, different lines and an inevitable crunch on the tight turns. We decided that I'd do three laps leading and try and shake him off, then he'd do three laps and try and shake me off. I was quite convinced that Deltapig wouldn't last six laps before exploding anyway.

Thrapping off the line and round the first corner, I glanced over my shoulder to see Deltapig following. It actually looks quite intimidating from the front, especially when viewed from the low-slung seat of the Mog. I hoped that Mark hadn't taken my piss-taking to heart; I had laid it on a bit thick. I slung it round the Molehill chicane then waited an age for the understeer to abate before booting it out of the long Fradley corner and down the straight, where I had time to check on Deltapig's position. Mark was a few lengths behind me on the straight, so I braked a bit later and a lot harder, then round for another lap. I was pulling away.

The weight distribution was a bit off, my own weight added about 15% to the weight of the vehicle, making right-handers grippier than left-handers. Through Molehill again, I tried leaning over to shift the weight about, which helped a bit, motorbike and sidecar style. It is so easy to run out of revs though and I thought of Mark's meticulous steering inputs and quick gear changes as I fought to build a respectable distance between us. The people watching were eating chips (bought with their winnings?) and the smell briefly distracted me: I braked late, locked up and Deltapig was on me again.

I made a cheeky tactical move. My mate Tipex jumped in to give me a bit of balance. The understeer was still evident, but the weight distribution was better and it slewed through the Molehill chicane in a more manageable fashion. The M3W pulled out a decent lead. Time to change. Mark set off first and, immediately, my concentration evaporated watching the 'pig ahead of me. Smoke was billowing off the rear tyres as bodywork scrubbed rubber, it lurched and lunged around corners and I was comfortably on his bumper for all three laps. The M3W wins on paper, and on track, but Deltapig really is insane. I had to lift my visor to wipe the tears of laughter from my eyes. What kind of lunatic chops up an already dynamically flawed vehicle, adds lots of power and then *races* it?

I shook hands with Mark in the paddock and saluted his engineering ingenuity/lunacy [delete as applicable]. Spectators' bets were off. With lungs full of the stench of burnt rubber, tears in our eyes and a head full of *"Three wheels on my wagon"*, neither of us could decide who the *real* winner was either.

Chasing the ambulance chasers: part 1

I am often asked how I find time to do all this stuff. My standard reply is: "I work very quickly and to a poor standard". This is only half-joking. If I can cut a corner, I will, and if I'm bored, I cannot stop my mind from wandering off somewhere more interesting. Earlier in my career, I used to fight this instinct, trying to focus on paying the bills, keeping my kids fed and watered, and the Halifax's bailiffs from knocking on my door. Nowadays, I can't fight this mental mischief and, if work keeps me at a desk, I need to find an outlet for it.

I had a lengthy spell in the office with nothing but coffee and the Internet for company. At that time, the 'no win, no fee' accident claims lawyers were feasting on everyone's bad fortune. Insurance premiums were rocketing and every scumbag who had so much as a supermarket scuff was claiming compensayshun [sic] for whiplash. The government has since changed the law thankfully, but back then, 'whiplash lawyers' would pay a referral fee for potential claims cases. This meant endless cold calls, spam emails and adverts everywhere; "have you had an accident?" I decided to have some fun with that.

The claims companies usually had an 'online chat' function. They would prefer you to call, or email, but as they all chased every potential claim in search of a lucrative referral fee, they had a chat function with which you could discuss your details if you'd been in an accident. These were, it seemed, manned by people who typed with two fingers and had no legal qualifications. All they wanted was confirmation you'd had an accident that wasn't your fault and your phone number. At the end of the chat, the transcript could be saved. At times, I laughed so hard stringing these parasites along that I had tears and snot all over my face. People visiting the office must have thought I loved that desk job. I have dozens of these transcripts, all 100% genuine and done under a nom de plume. Here are a couple of my favourites.

Please wait for a site operator to respond.

You are now chatting with 'Barry'

Barry: Hello. Im your Claims Direct chat representative . How can I help you?

ben: hi i had an accident and need 2 no how 2 claim

Barry: Could you tell me a little more about what has happened?

ben: yes. i was in the works van and had an accident. question is, does the other person need to be insured 4 me 2 claim?

Barry: Sometimes but we can also look at it through the motor insurance bureau.

Barry: It would be best if we discussed this further over the phone, could you provide a telephone number?

ben: the other guy won't be on the insurance database, i know that

Barry: If he is not insured then we could claim through the motor insurance bureau.

ben: OK. how does that work tho, he wasnt in a car ?

Barry: It would be better to discuss it over the phone, could you provide a telephone number/

ben: I don't have his number, he can't even speak, he just ran out into the road.

Barry: In this case then we would not be able to pursue a claim for you.

ben: Surely the chimp who hit me must have some insurance ? someone is responsible for him ?

Barry: If you were able to find that out then, we would be able to pursue a claim. If not then we could not help you.

ben: I have that. Dudley Manor Park and Zoo. It just sprinted out the gate and under my wheels. Made a right mess of the van. It just went 'oo-oo-aa-aa' before it passed out. I don't know if that was through pain or if that was it's normal voice.

Barry: We would not be able to help you with that

ben: Why?

Barry: Thank you for chatting. Good-bye.

Chat session has been terminated by the site operator.

Please wait for a site operator to respond.

You are now chatting with 'Alison'

Alison: Good Evening, Welcome to National Accident helpline chat. I am a legally trained advisor here, how can I help you?

MARY MULLIGAN: GOOD EVENIN I AM MARY MULLIGAN. I NEED HELP BECAUSE OF AN ACIDENT.

Please wait while I transfer the chat to 'Kerri.'.

You are now chatting with 'Kerri.'

MARY MULLIGAN: HELLO ALISON. ARE YOU THERE?

Kerri.: sorry how can i help?

MARY MULLIGAN: WHAT HAPPENED TO ALISON? DID I DO SOMETHING WRONG? I NEED ADVISE ON MY ACIDENT.

Kerri.: im sorry it was the end of her shift but i can help.

MARY MULLIGAN: I NEED SOME HELP BECAUSE OF THE ACIDENT I HAD.

Kerri.: ok what sort of accident did you have?

MARY MULLIGAN: A TRANSIT VAN DROVE INTO MY HOME. I GOT VERY BADLY HURT.

Kerri.: im really sorry to hear that. When did this happen?

MARY MULLIGAN: 3 DAYS AGO. WE STILL CLEARIN UP.

Kerri.: and what sort of injuries have you suffered?

MARY MULLIGAN: FACIAL MAINLY (ON FACE)

Kerri.: .have you been to the hosptial then?

MARY MULLIGAN: NO. HUSBAND WONT LET ME AS HE DOESNT WANT TROUBLE FOR THE CRASH

Kerri.: was it your husband that caused the accident then?

MARY MULLIGAN: NO NOT DIRECTLY

Kerri.: have the police been involved at all?

MARY MULLIGAN: JESUS, NO, THEYD WANT TO SEARCH THE CARAVEN

MARY MULLIGAN: WE LIVE IN THE CARAVEN, ON THE A6 LAYBY

Kerri.: in order to take a claim forward we would need to know who was at fault. Do you have details of the person that hit into you?

MARY MULLIGAN: YES.

MARY MULLIGAN: WILL YOU WANT TO LOOK INSIDE THE CARAVEN? IM NOT ALLOWED 2 LET ANYONE IN IT.

MARY MULLIGAN: ACTUALLY THERES NOT MUCH LEFT OF IT ANYWAY

Kerri.: is it a caravan or a motor home?

MARY MULLIGAN: IT WAS A TRANSIT VAN AND A CARAVAN

Kerri.: ok can i ask if you have a postcode?

MARY MULLIGAN: I DONT NO THE FULL ONE. IT STARTS NN18 I THINK.

Kerri.: can you except mail?

MARY MULLIGAN: 'EXCEPT' OR 'ACCEPT' ?

Kerri.: we need an address to send mail too and to put you in touch with a solicitor based on a postcode.

MARY MULLIGAN: I SEE. YES. YOU CAN DELIVER US A LETTER. WE'LL KEEP THE DOG INSIDE WHEN YOU COME.

Kerri.: we do not deliver mail personally it is all done through mail and phone but we need a full uk postcode so we can put you with

the right solicitor.

MARY MULLIGAN: YES YES. WE HAVE THAT. WE GET LETTERS FROM THE COUNCIL ALL THE TIME.

Kerri.: ok are you able to find the full postcode now?

MARY MULLIGAN: I HAVE IT, TRY "NN17 4ET" IN CORBY

Kerri.: is it the industrial estate?

MARY MULLIGAN: YES! WE'RE IN THEIR CARPARK NOW. COUNCIL GAVE US 6 WEEKS.

MARY MULLIGAN: SPIOL INDUSTRY IS THE DOOR.

Kerri.: ok do you have a phone number and we can get someone to call you and explain how the process works?

MARY MULLIGAN: OK. DONT U JUST POST THE MONEY?

Kerri.: no we need you to speak to a solicitor first and then they would investigate everything and depending on your injuries they

would be able to tell you how much compensation you are entitled too?

MARY MULLIGAN: OH. CAN I TALK TO ALISON INSTEAD? I PREFERRED HER. I FELT THAT I WAS MORE LIKELY TO EARN COMPENSAYSHUN FROM HER THAN YOU. I ONLY NEED ENOUGH MONEY TO GET THE DOG SPAYED AND PADDYS TEETH FIXED. AND SOME DIESEL FOR THE VAN. £25 SHOULD DO IT. I DONT CARE THAT IT PUTS EVERYONE ELSES INSURANCE UP AS A RESULT. FECK THE LOT OF EM. I RECKON YOU COMPENSAYSHUN PEOPLE ARE LIKE US TRAVELLERS A BIT, DON'T YOU? LESS POPULAR THAN US, OBVIOUSLY AND WITH FEWER MORALS. CAN I TALK TO ALISON AGAIN OR WILL U JUST SEND A CHECK? LET ME KNOW WHEN YOURE COMING AND I'LL PUT THE DOGS INSIDE, THEYLL BITE YOUR FACE OFF IF THEYRE NOT TIED UP.

Kerri.: im afraid we can no longer help. Good bye

MARY MULLIGAN: IF YOU DONT SEND US THE MONEY WE'LL PUT A CURSE ON YOUR HOLE FAMILY. AND YOUR DOG. IF YOU HAVE ONE. IF NOT WE'LL CURSE ANY DOMESTIC PET YOU HAVE. APART FROM FISH COS THAT DONT WORK. YOU CANT CURSE FISH. THEY CANT REMEMBER ANYTHING.

Kerri.: thankyou and goodbye

MARY MULLIGAN: WANT ANY PEGS ?

Chat session has been terminated by the site operator.

Applecross in an Abarth

Car;   Rented Abarth 500. A proper old-school hot hatch, with bonus scorpions.

Location;   Inverness, then Applecross, Scotland.

Duration;   24 hours plus flights there and back.

The destination of Inverness isn't quite as glamorous as others in this book, but it is the nearest airport to the Applecross pass, which, if you call it by it's Gaelic name of 'Bealach na Bà', makes you feel like you are abroad after all. Some would argue that Scotland *is* abroad for an Englishman, but as long as the currency, lingo and laws on driving are the same, I'll class it as not abroad. On the subject of Scotland, why do you never see 'wee' Jimmy Krankie in the same room as Scottish nationalist Nicola Sturgeon? I digress. easyJet from England to Inverness doesn't take long and a return flight cost £38—less than it would cost me in petrol and in a fraction of the time it would take to drive there.

Using skills honed on previous trips, I smugly collected the keys to an Abarth 500 at Inverness' airport car rental desk, remembering to tick the 'super extra insurance cover' box as usual, while my fellow automotive adventurers were saddled with 1.2 Corsas. How did I blag such an interesting car? I spotted it in their car park on a previous trip, made my booking for a standard car online, then called the desk at the airport direct a few days before arrival and said I'd like the Abarth please and would bring them all a present if they could help. Dead easy. A tenner spent on two large tins of Quality Street and the little cracker was mine. The Abarth is, essentially, a posh Fiat 500 with a 1.4 turbo'd engine, lots of scorpion logos and an interior blacker than a goth convention in a coal mine. I made sure to never leave the keys out of my sight, as those thugs in 1.2 Corsas were not to be trusted.

The sun was shining, incredible for the time of year, so I set off heading in the direction of Loch Ness and the start of the A87. This road was once voted the best biker's road in the UK. I can see why. No cameras, no traffic and the possibility to build up healthy speeds through long flowing corners on perfect tarmac amongst the mountains. It was easy to lose the Corsas, but the few locals we encountered seemed happy to overtake everyone regardless at 100+ mph. Here, if you have an accident, it's likely that you'll know the other party somehow. Tight-knit communities where people help one another and hit-and-runs are uncommon. It reminds me of Iceland, a country with very little drink-driving because the population is so small that everyone knows everyone else and no one wants a reputation. If you get it wrong here, everyone will know.

We made a quick stop at Eilean Donan Castle, named after Donnán of Eigg, a Celtic saint martyred in 617 for trying to introduce Christianity. There are some brilliant old tales of uprisings and clan feuds here, one culminating with the memorable line "an aggrieved Maclennan apparently shot MacMhurchaidh in the buttocks with an arrow". In the early 19th century, the castle was briefly held by "an Irishman, a captain, a Spanish lieutenant, a serjeant, one Scotch rebel and 39 Spanish soldiers", who promptly surrendered when the Royal Navy turned up. The castle looks ancient but was rebuilt in 1919 by the gloriously titled Lieutenant Colonel John MacRae-Gilstrap after the Royal Navy used 27 barrels of gunpowder to

blow it to smithereens. What fun that must have been!
Our entertainment lay up the road.

We came to the bottom of the Applecross pass as the sun
began to set. Locals say that it's Gaelic name 'Bealach na
Bà' means 'pass of the cattle', but I think it actually means
'eaten by midges', as at certain times of the year, the
bastard things feast on visiting *sassenachs* like me.
Applecross is considered the UK's only Alpine pass and
the roads, views and potential for thrilling driving aren't
far off those found in the Alps thousands of miles south
from here. But we had a problem. Firstly, in addition to
the midges, every time I stopped, I was assaulted by Corsa
drivers trying to mug me for my keys. Secondly, the
bloody road was closed. This was a biggy. I had been
tipped off that there were roadworks and that the pass
might be shut, but only after I'd booked my flight and car.
Some ingenuity was required to drive the bit of road we'd
come so very far to enjoy. I did not want to be the one to

move the barriers in case we got caught doing it. I threw my keys over the steel barriers blocking the road and the animals accompanying me pulled the barrier aside and down the hillside in their scramble to get their hands on what they thought were my Abarth keys. They were my house keys. Road now reopened, without my fingerprints on any evidence, I drove into the sunset and around the first few hairpins, ignoring the warning signs about the weather.

The road is really narrow. One car wide in most places and the little Abarth filled the road. It's slightly elevated in places too, meaning you can't drop a wheel off the tarmac. In sections, it is cut into the mountainside and the views of the sun setting were magical. Admiring this, and trying not to fall off the road, I nearly missed the colossal hole in the road. I had sort of hoped we could drive around the roadworks on the pavement or something, but there was no pavement—there was a huge hole in the mountainside like a bomb had gone off. Below is a picture of a picture that a local later showed me of the hole in daylight.

Work should have been at a more advanced stage I was told, but the ground was frozen so they'd given up. Three-point turning little rental cars is normally a doddle, but on a road two inches wider than the car is long, and a drop-off into a peaty bog, it became an exercise in wheel-twirling and hand-shuffling. As our little convoy shuffled round, a light came on in a nearby field and out of the gloom came a dumper truck with a very angry-looking man shouting at us. Back-forwards-back-forwards... eventually, the Abarth was pointing back down the hill and we had the most one-sided car chase in history as we scampered off leaving what must have been the security or site manager way behind. We thoughtfully put the barriers back as we passed because, believe it or not, we wouldn't want anyone to come a cropper.

Our overnight stay was at the Applecross Inn, just over the mountainside that we had found closed. The alternative route was 30 miles around the coast on a road that, on my map, was scarcely wider than a pubic hair. This road was thoroughly entertaining. Endless dips and tight turns on a gritty surface with the odd pothole and glorious views of the moon over the sea for the odd nanosecond you dare take your eye off the screaming Corsa in front. Real roller coaster roads. There is always an element of 'pressing on' in these conditions. The speed limit is, mostly, 60 mph, but you'd have to be braver than McRae to do that in the daylight, let alone in the pitch black. I had a hard time focussing on the Corsa in front, even though I had considerably more power and the advantage of being the following car, watching his lines. Being on the limit on public roads is a silly business, but I wasn't far from it. At that point, I saw the interior light come on in the Corsa in front and the driver held a map in one hand and drove, surely blinded by the light, with the other, maintaining the same frenetic pace. I'm no rally God. I didn't want to drive like this any more. We backed off.

The Applecross Inn is a fantastic place to stay: the food, drink, views and ambiance are spot-on. I even pretended to like whisky. It's bloody fortunate it is good though, as you're a long way from a Travelodge up there. I had a skinful and the company was great. My mate Carlos, sloshed, was describing the fun of the drive. "Did you see them things on the road?", he rambled, in his Mancunian accent. "You know, them big hairy bastards?" We were at a loss. The barman chipped in; "They're sheep".

Waking up with a heavy head (must have been the scallops), we zipped up the Applecross pass from the west. The road was clear and dry but the air quickly got colder as we climbed up the tight road. It wasn't long before the TCS light was blinking away. Nothing to do with fritzy Italian electrics though, there was thick ice on shady corners. At the top of the pass was a smattering of virgin snow, the closure meaning we were the only people there. I fell out of the car; icy Scottish mountainside is no place for poncy driving shoes. It surprised me how much grip the 'Fiat in a posh frock' had. The vista at the top over Raasay toward Skye is simply stunning, although nearly every corner we turned on the entire trip had a view the Scottish tourist board should be proud of. The people we met were most friendly. None of them shot me in the arse with an arrow, even though my driving might have deserved it.

Time was tight for the return flight. We took the road that joined up with the A896 and stopped to liberate my stomach of the previous night's session near Strathcarron. As I sat in a ditch, retching, I realised that the name of this little place was familiar. In the late 1990s, Lord Strathcarron had founded a car company in his own name, a Lotus Elise-alike machine originally designed to be powered by a motorbike engine, but a change in rules meant they were forced out of business before production started. Lord Strathcarron went on to write a book called "Mysticism and Bliss". It *is* blissful up here. Even in a ditch covered in your own sick. Time for the A832 to Inverness and the flight back home.

I was a bit sad to give the Abarth 500 back. Scorpion beat Griffin for entertainment. It was plenty quick enough in a straight line and looks rather funky, but is easily unsettled on the twisties thanks to a short wheelbase, oversized wheels and bouncy rear suspension. Driving one quickly is hard work—it feels like an old-school hot hatch. For that feeling alone, I loved it, and loved my trip to Scotland. When I got home, I had to break in. My house keys are still in the heather on the mountainside of Applecross somewhere.

A(n alcoholic) lap of Goodwood

Car;   None. Transport this time was a second-hand pair of size 8s.

Location;   Glorious Goodwood, England.

Duration;   One day's tomfoolery, plus a day either side enjoying the event.

I love the Goodwood Revival. But, despite firing off a broadside of begging letters, it became apparent that no one was prepared to lend me a priceless classic to participate in some racing. The cars, the people, the atmosphere, the aircraft and the music. I love it all. Even if Ferrari *had* coughed over some keys to a 250 GTO, our lack of celeb credentials meant we wouldn't be rubbing chrome with Rowan Atkinson and that fat northern chef. Thingy. What's-his-face.

Sat in the press tent (pic) watching the real journos hammer out race reports you've probably read standing up in WHSmith, my old mate Dr. Octane and I hatched a plan combining our two favourite things; drinking and racing. Starting in the press tent, we were to each take a drink in every single location around the circumference of the circuit, the winner being the first person to reach the finish line of the Speckled Hen tent.

The man from Ferrari Fawning Weekly kindly dropped the flag and we burst out of the tent and took a hard right, both Dr. O and I sauntered through the paddock of vintage racers. Yes, sauntered. Neither of us was going to show a lack of decorum by actually *running*; PE is a sweaty and unpleasant business, and I have successfully avoided it since leaving school all those years ago. This race would be won on cunning, guile and bladder capacity. My first stop was the Veuve Clicquot tent for a cold glass of bubbly. This took longer than hoped for, as I insisted on a real glass and not a plastic beaker.

I had already lost Dr. O. Perhaps he had been refused entry; his tweed did have the unmistakeable aroma of charity shop. I had gone purple in the first sector. I loosened my worsted tie and took a good chug of port and brandy from my hip flask. A press pass means entry to the paddocks, away from the general public, and a slightly shorter route to the next drink. I did not consider this to be exceeding track limits. Here, I almost bumped into Keith Chegwin. After exchanging apologies and enquiring if he was enjoying the Revival, I shook his hand and said, "How very nice to meet you, Keith". At this point, Keith visibly wilted and his smile dropped. That was because he wasn't Keith Chegwin. He was Noel Edmonds.

From here, I needed to head to the outfield, so back through the crowds and under the tunnel on the Lavant Straight and down to the Lavant Corner bar for a pint of Guinness. Glug. Then a long left to St Mary's, hugging the apex, for another Guinness, where I was served quickly while other drinkers were watching a Spitfire. From here was the long slog down Madgwick, but I was struggling for grip in my army surplus shoes and had a stitch. As I ambled along, Dr. O. passed, having hitched a lift on the tractor bus service, sailing into an unsporting lead. Schumacher-esque behaviour. A pint at Madgwick, then power walking through the crowds to Woodcote for another. Feeling gassy now, I had to slacken off my Sam Browne. Room for a G&T. The rules did not specify the type of alcohol to be consumed and I was already more bloated than an off-season Montoya.

Press passes are not given out willy-nilly. You'll often need a copy of your public liability insurance (or a copy of someone else's nicked off the 'net, and hope you don't have or cause an accident), copies of previously published work (or someone else's work with your name photoshopped on) and other paperwork. Events like this attract a massive crowd and they, rightly, only want the best coverage from the best writers and photographers. My attitude is that everyone else will cover the conventional stuff far more professionally than I ever could. I won't have the first pics of the day online, I won't spot the rarest car there and my style of writing is barely fit for this book, let alone the pages of Ferrari Fawning Monthly. So I have to find a unique angle, do something different, like this drunken race against the backdrop of motor racing.

The end was in sight. Over the pedestrian footbridge into the 'over the road' section for half a Guinness, then stopping for a breather at the Chap Olympiad, who were performing their moustache tug-o-war.

Where was Dr. O? His bladder had almost ruptured and he had been obliged to pit. I spotted him as he exited the latrines, fiddling with his flies and staggering down the steps in what was surely an unsafe release. Our paths converged towards the finish line, the bar of the Speckled Hen tent, both wanting to win, neither wanting to cheat by running. My straight line turned into an arc as my internal gyroscope fought with the effects of an afternoon's binge drinking. Nearly there! I was momentarily distracted by a beautiful blonde in a red dress and Dr. O nipped in for the win. I forced a consolatory pint down.

A footnote to this chapter. I got blacklisted by Goodwood when they heard about this drunken lap and the blonde and I became an item. I *love* the Revival.

Barnstorming: part 2

Car;	Lotus Exige S V6; simplicate and add madness.
Location;	Another deserted airfield, England.
Duration;	6 hours.

When it comes to cars, I usually prefer British. That's not to say I believe that just because a car is made in Britain I think it is automatically better than foreign alternatives. It is because the kind of car I love isn't really made by anyone else. Morgans with their leather, wood and occasional wonkiness are unique in the modern age. Caterham seem to take 1950s racing car technology and make it *just about* acceptable in the modern world. I recall the entire roof of a brand new Caterham coming off at speed on the motorway and blowing into a nearby field. When I told Caterham they said, "yeah, they *do* tend to do that—anyway, did you enjoy yourself?" And I did. I really did. The roof is only a little bit of cheap vinyl anyway and the car made me feel like Stirling Moss. Another British manufacturer I love, warts and all, is Lotus.

There is a common theme here. Fans of flawless Japanese machinery or dependable German marques might be less charitable than me, but it's not to do with trim quality. It's to do with innovation. These uniquely British marques are all born from necessity. The need to produce performance with little development budgets, using materials others might ignore or techniques no one had thought of. Lotus is a great example of that. A company like this is a reflection of it's creator and Colin Chapman was typical of men who lived through the make-do-and-mend years of the war, who worked in Britain's aviation industry where things had to be light and strong and produced quickly and without dozens of rubber stamps. The men behind Marcos, Cosworth and others who ended up in F1 all had the creativity that comes from having naff-all money and a single-minded desire to build something that beats the rest. Lotus makes fast, light and thrilling sports cars that no one else seems to do, even today. The phrase "Simplicate, and add lightness" was attributed to William Bushnell Stout, an American aircraft designer, but was best associated with Lotus.

The aircraft tie-in seemed appropriate and the car had to be a Lotus. Following my earlier barnstorming fun, I wanted to try it again, but in something quicker. The most agile, responsive and exciting of aircraft I could access versus the same, in car form; a Lotus Exige S V6. This was (at the time) the fastest car they'd ever built, and I had successfully scrounged one. A bonded aluminium tub, plastic panels and a supercharged 3.5 litre V6 engine from Toyota. Detractors of British cars might say that Lotus cars are often a bit of a bodge—but the results are remarkable. 0–60 mph in 3.8 seconds in addition to ride quality, steering feel and braking that are all best-in-class. But this isn't an advertorial. The key fob looks to me like it comes from an E46 BMW. The wiper and indicator stalks are from a mid-90s Vauxhall Cavalier and those wing mirrors are from a Rover Metro. I don't care. They were all chosen because they're simple and robust. They all fit with Lotus' "Simplicate, and add lightness" mantra. The plane it was up against was a CAP 231, designed specifically for aerobatics, piloted by a friend who I cannot name, but will call Bob.

The CAP 231 weighs 720 kg and is powered by a Lycoming air-cooled flat six with 300 hp. The Exige V6S weighs 1170 kg and has 345 bhp. The plane would hit 248 mph versus the Lotus' 170 mph. Also, I can't drive for toffee. The plane would be quicker and Bob thought it would be rather one-sided. Bob has the same genes, the same gung-ho attitude and the same sense of adventure that the men who design my favourite British cars have. So we agreed, in the name of a fair fight, that he would fly inverted, and as low as he dared. The Exige accelerates like a twatted golf ball, so when he crossed the airfield's perimeter hedge, I'd stand on the gas and we'd see who got to the end of the runway first. He'd then bank round and run again. Neither of us would cheat; we'd run until we hit the perfectly timed start, then scream down the runway. Why? Oh do come on, do we *really* need a reason to race the fastest car Lotus had ever made versus a stunt plane?

This time, the security manager could not be bribed. Well, he probably could, but the HSE representative was visiting and would be on site doing an assessment. That, really, should have been enough for us to change dates, but it's not easy to get a stunt plane pilot, stunt plane, car and driver all in the same place, on a day that isn't too rainy or windy, so we'd thought we'd wing it. Ahem. We had a safety briefing. Bob didn't bother mentioning that he'd be upside down and I didn't bother mentioning we had no insurance. Lotus thought we were doing a photo shoot. Colin Chapman was an aircraft fanatic and I would like to think that he would have approved of our fun. He was infamous for rule bending. In an excellent biography of him by Mike Lawrence ("Wayward genius", find it on Amazon), there are some great examples of this. I particularly liked him saving weight and trying to get around scrutineers who insisted on a metal bulkhead in racing cars by using a cardboard bulkhead painted in aluminium-based paint, therefore (just about) complying with the rule. When the tax rules changed on self-assembly cars, such as his Lotus 7, he insisted his was not a self-assembly car and instead provided his customers with a *disassembly* manual—and a note saying that they should read it in reverse. He must have been a pain in the arse to the authorities but, my word, he got things done.

The Exige is the only car I have ever driven that made me drive like a complete arsehole. I am known for pootling along to BBC Radio 6 letting the world whizz by me on the open road. I have enough adventures without having to misbehave in public. The Exige makes you want to overtake everything, everywhere, *all the time*. There is no elasticity in the acceleration, no inertia, just *whump* and you're past whatever was in front. The steering feel and grip seemingly encourage you to scythe around corners at very silly speeds with confidence. But that's not to say it's a yobbo's car. It doesn't seem to attract the negative attention that something like a Porsche might. People love Lotus. There's a whiff of underdog about it. The sills are so wide, the seats so low and the door aperture so small that you need a particular technique to get in and out gracefully. And you'll still kick the speaker getting in. Rear three-quarter visibility is terrible. The engine is noisy. Geeks will play spot-the-parts-bin switchgear and no one will be impressed with the nasty-looking head unit. And then you start it; it is noisy. The controls are light, everything is simple, you pull away and before you know it, you're rocketing along. I've driven an S1 Exige too, the one with the stupidly highly strung Rover K-series engine in it, but this later model feels much beefier, despite having the same "Simplicate, and add lightness" design criteria.

Bob is one of those gifted, laid-back types, relying on flair and creativity to solve problems if they arise instead of wasting hours and days planning for events that would probably never happen. This meant Bob spent the safety briefing smoking and nodding while clearly thinking of something else. He is tall, scrawny and usually daydreaming about something more interesting than what he is actually doing. I smiled and signed things in the name of Duisberg, which is a nom de plume that Mr. HSE never bothered to check and I never bothered to tell him that any legal claims would be against a fictitious name supposedly residing at an empty factory unit nowhere near where I actually live. People sometimes ask me, how do I dare get away with these things? It's surprisingly easy. You do it on the basis you won't have an accident, won't get caught and are in a car quick enough to escape should it all go tits up. Or tits down, I suppose, if you're speaking from the perspective of an inverted stunt plane. There is nothing to stop you, or anyone else, from doing this. It's just a matter of how much you want to do it, and being creative enough to allow it to happen. It's something I learned from reading about Colin Chapman, Your Honour.

"Runway clear", said the miserable bastard in the tower. It was clear they didn't want us there, but we were. We had paid the fee for site access for "flyby photography" and they had to let us in. In the Lotus was a walkie-talkie to the tower and another radio handset to talk to Bob who, bored waiting for us to be in position, was loop-the-looping over the East Midlands countryside above our heads. There was also a mobile phone gaffa-taped to the dash on loudspeaker. The first run went badly. The timing was OK but the plane was too far from the car. "Mate, this isn't a race if you're quarter of a mile away". He banked, we put the car back in place and went again. This time, the distraction of being so close seemed to slow Bob down and, as he drew near, I simply stood on the accelerator pedal; 1st, 2nd, 3rd and, before I knew it, I was out of runway with the plane far behind. It's not hard to drive very quickly in a straight line, but watching over your shoulder and also judging your braking point before you end up in the turnips is not easy. We nailed it the third time.

The HSE guy was watching now; "What the f*ck are you playing at?!", he shouted. "I can't talk", said Bob, nonchalantly, "I'm a bit upside down". Unfortunately, I had left my radio switched on and HSE man heard me laughing and got even angrier, even over the noise of the whiney supercharged V6 behind my head. We were called in to the tower for a talking-to.

It's easier to ask forgiveness than permission; this is a motto that usually serves me well, but not here. He was really, really angry. Bob had switched off. HSE man was furious and wanted us off the site. He wanted paperwork we didn't have and explanations we couldn't give. I was grinning. I had barnstormed an Exige against a stunt plane. Nothing could take that experience away. A stunting CAP aircraft of a very similar specification had suffered structural failure and crashed a couple of years earlier, killing the pilot, he said. "Oh. Yeah", said Bob who knew this already and was almost certainly a friend of the deceased anyway. I didn't understand this method of bollocking. If anyone died, it would be Bob. Yes, he might hit me too, or someone else, but he'd be the first to go in the event of an accident. The potential for an accident lies in his hands, literally. Upside down, there is nothing but a thin Perspex canopy between his happy face and the tarmac a few metres away. HSE man had to report something and told us to wait while he made a phone call.

We quickly agreed to scarper. Bob had to refuel. In the real world of aviation, this means paying some bloke cash and you screw a fat hose into your aircraft and fill up while he watches. I opened the gate and drove the Lotus off the runway with a "Lotus has left the runway" over the radio to the man in the tower who, even at this distance, was gesticulating to indicate that I am a masturbator. Bob, sat on the steps of the tanker, lit a cigarette in the haze of avgas, the HSE man returned and looked like he was giving birth. I don't doubt that he plays a vital role in ensuring this little airfield in the middle of nowhere is safe. I also don't doubt that, had we obeyed his instructions, this very British stunt would never have happened.

Targa Florio

Car;	Rented Fiat 500 1.2 petrol. Bouncy, bouncy.
Location;	Sicily, Italy.
Duration;	24 hours there, plus half a day's travel either side.

The trackday business in the UK is booming. For £100 upwards, you can spend a day on a closed circuit, in a relatively safe environment, enjoying the performance of your car. Some circuits, of course, are more interesting than others. My favourite UK circuits are Donington and Cadwell, but I've driven most and none are more than a few miles long. I think the Silverstone GP circuit is perhaps the longest at just over 3 miles. It's flat too, and for all the excitement of pushing yourself to go faster, the scenery gets a bit repetitive after a few roundy rounds. And there's the inevitable wear and tear on your car, even if you don't prang it. For just about the same budget, you can fly easyJet to Palermo, rent a little hatchback for a day and enjoy one of the world's longest and most fascinating circuits; the Targa Florio.

I had no idea what the wizened little old man was saying, but he was clearly extremely angry. We had climbed over a fence and he had caught us, fair do's, but I had the feeling that it wasn't his fence or his grandstand that he was living under and, therefore, we were no better than him. "Targa Florio", I said, trying to explain myself. More shouting, a bit less waving and a few threatening steps towards me. He had a face like a big raisin, tanned from the Mediterranean sun, topped by a black beret. He was wearing two shirts, two holey jumpers and his jeans were help up with rope. As he berated me for whatever, the spineless gits I was with climbed back over the fence behind him, leaving me to a bollocking in a language I knew nothing of. I had only wanted a photograph of the bust of the man who had brought us here, Vincenzo Florio, which stood between the semi-derelict grandstands in the hills of Sicily. "Photo. Targa Florio", I said, holding out my arms and doing the international mime for driving. He held out his hands and did the international mime for begging. "Money's in the car!", I lied, and climbed back over the wobbly wire fence, snagging my trousers on the way back over, before driving off at speed. Florio made his money in the wine trade, married a princess and brought a crocodile home from his honeymoon. He was inspired by the Gordon Bennett races elsewhere in Europe and decided to found a race in his own name; the Targa Florio. There's a history here that no circuit in England can match.

It was good to be back in a Fiat 500. You never quite know which keys you'll get at the rental desk, but in Italy, a 500 seemed most appropriate. It's a cheap and simple hatchback and, in this impoverished part of Italy in particular, perfect for the job. Many original 500s are still in daily use here, it's relatively warm and dry and, unless you're a mafia don or politician (or both), then chances are you won't be able to afford anything newer. Italians buy cars, rag them to death and then throw them away.

How the original 500s stood up to atrocious roads and lunatic drivers I will never know, but they do, and the roads are more interesting because of it. Piaggio Apes too. Ape (pronounced ah-pay) is the Italian for bee, and the name comes from the drone of these weird and ancient moped-based, three-wheeled delivery vans. I'd love an Ape or a 500 in my garage at home in England, but suspect the damp here would turn them to a scruffy pile of ferrous oxide in a week or two. The new 500, bouncy little machine, is great fun, and we charged off down the pit lane to a full lap of the original Targa Florio route, map taped to the dash, angry squatter/beggar man still shouting.

The whole route is public road. All of it. Some might say even the pit lanes and grandstands are public too, for this is Italy where no one quite seems to know the rules and a backhander seems to change the rules in your favour. Cerda is the nearest town and the circuit starts nearby. The faded signage, pits, tower, bridge and grandstand are all deserted bar the occasional beggar and fly-tipper (more on that later). If you look carefully, you might see the occasional original and sun-bleached yellow road sign with "Targa Florio" marking the route. The inaugural race on these same public roads (much of it dirt tracks back then) was a single, 92-mile loop held in 1906. There were, depending on how you count them, approximately 2000 corners. In comparison, the longest variation of the next-best-thing, Germany's Nürburgring, had 180. Local knowledge is king and you'll find 'NINO' and 'VV' in white paint on walls and barns in the mountains here. 'Viva Vaccarella' was the message for the local teacher, Nino Vaccarella, who won here three times. The history of the racing seems so close, so genuine, that there's a little museum somewhere but the thrill is in bouncing down the same empty roads, following the route, with the tumbledown villages seemingly having changed little in over a century. From 1948 to 1950, the route took in an almost complete lap of the island, all 670 miles of it, on one single, colossal lap. Our trip, though, is on the circuit used from 1951 to 1977, when racing here ended. Vaccarella still lives here and it's not hard to find him, although my email asking to see him went unanswered. To be fair, he's in his eighties and I like to think he's still charging about these mountains all day in his retirement in some scabby Lancia.

Cerda had policemen with assault rifles on the road in, and out, of town. This is mafia country. It was explained to me that, here, far from Rome and Milan, people have to fend for themselves. You might not like it but the local mafia will provide assistance that politicians cannot. There's the feeling of not knowing quite who is who or what the ground rules are. The countryside is beautiful, but at nearly every place we stopped to let the poor screaming Fiat catch it's breath, there were piles of rotting litter. I've seen the same near Napoli.

The mafia love the EU. The EU means bureaucracy, well-paid officials and a steady stream of money. The mafia control many recycling contracts with the local councils, and it is far easier to dump the rubbish in the hills than it is to actually recycle it. Wikipedia reckons 70% of Sicilian businesses pay protection money to the mafia and that it costs the local economy €10 billion a year. Old man Ferrari looked down his nose at Sicily, considering it rural and uncouth. Yet he, like other manufacturers, fought hard to build cars that would be victorious here, winning a total of seven times and finishing behind Alfa Romeo on ten and Porsche on eleven occasions.

Up into the mountains we went. Cypress trees, views of Mount Etna and stone walls with 'VV' scrawled on them. The higher we went, the worse the road surface became, but we couldn't slow down. Alessandro Cagno set the fastest lap in 1906, at a speed of 30mph, and I wanted to beat that if I could. Cagno lived to a ripe old age, unusual for a man who raced cars hard, competed in powerboats and was a pioneer of early bombing for the fledgling Italian Air Force. He said, "*due to the roads, the rules, the tires changes, the trivial incidents, the crashes, our races exposed us to a hard labour, starting at 5 in the morning, till the afternoon... a lot of drawbacks, off the road, not asphalted roads, wheel changes, sacrifices of personal needs*". Racing back then was an incredibly courageous thing to do—we were just mucking about in a hire car. But what fun.

The race was a huge success, it brought much needed tourism to this neglected corner of Italy and the crowds were huge. Vincenzo Florio would have been delighted that his race grew to be the most thrilling road race in the world for so many years. Locals loved it, there are still murals dedicated to the race, but they couldn't be trusted not to hinder foreign teams. Mercedes won in 1924, by quite a margin, but instead of their customary white paint scheme, they had the cars painted red, Italian colours, in order to confuse partisan spectators. One of the first instances of drivers doing a recce ahead of a long race happened here. The gifted Czech racer, Alžběta Pospíšilová (known as Elizabeth Junek), walked the entire course before the 1926 race and made pace notes. She ran in fourth place for some time before she crashed out. She actually lived to be 93, while many others perished here.

Above Caltavuturo, the tarmac's battle with subsidence was lost. It seemed smeared onto the road surface thinner and crumblier than you'd find elsewhere anyway, but the surface below had subsided and easily pulled the meagre blacktop apart. In your own car, you'd be three-point turning and looking for another route, but here, in a rental car, we were smashing over the ruts and holes like the racers of old. Ahead was a dark blue Punto with official-looking lights on it and a man in a pantomime uniform. Could be police, council, army… we had no idea. He was delighted to have someone to talk to on this remote road. "I am senior officer for the roads", he said in bad English. I wasn't sure what to do next. He couldn't be that important as he didn't have a gun. Was the road closed? Some flapping. "My car!", he said, proudly pointing at the immaculate but old Punto. "I am senior officer for the roads!" Can we pass? No answer. "Ees my car". Then, waving at the mountains. "Thees. I am senior officer for the roads." We're going to go now, thanks. Nice Punto. "Grazie! Grazie!" To this day, I have no idea what was going on.

The mountains were beautiful, but the course took us back down to sea level, 600 m below, and the Buonfornello straight. This straight is over 6 km longer than the Mulsanne straight at Le Mans. It meant that cars designed to compete in the Targa Florio would have weird gearing. Super-short for the hairpins and tight curves in the hills and a very long top gear for this super-high-speed straight. Leo Kinnunen set the fastest ever lap of Targa Florio in a Porsche 908 in 1970. A modest 79 mph. Considering the top speed of this car was nearly 100 mph faster, it shows the huge disparity in road conditions between the twisties up there and the mega straight down here. In '77, there was a whopping shunt at the end of this straight. God knows what terminal velocity they hit, but it ended racing here for good. Our 500 could have had another 5 miles and still struggled to hit three figures, even in kph.

We spent the night in Cefalù, an historic town on the coast. Our hotel was next to a bar, which, in turn, was next to a police station. The police station was empty, lights off. The bar was packed with policemen, in full uniform, armed to the teeth and drinking lots and lots of wine. Streets were tight and cobbled. Old Lancias and Fiats were the norm. The Piaggio Apes were so cool, in 70s shades of green, flatbeds with sacks of produce. Food in the restaurant was spectacularly good. There's much to recommend Cefalù: historic buildings, good food and a pretty little harbour.

Other Brits have been here; grade A fruitcake Aleister Crowley (pictured) established an occultist abbey here in the 1920s, but Benito Mussolini himself had it closed down in 1923 after a follower of Crowley called Raoul Loveday died after drinking cat's blood. This didn't put me off; after a day of hard driving, we were all ravenous. We ate octopus, pasta, fresh fish and enjoyed decent beer followed by grappa and got back to the hotel so late, we had to break in as they'd locked us out. We could sleep it off as tomorrow was an easy trip home, or so we thought.

"It's a bit black over Bill's mother's" is a phrase fellow East Midlanders will know means there's bad weather ahead. In the morning, with heavy heads, we had set off for the drive back to the airport, via Mount Etna, the active volcano in the heart of Sicily. At 3329 m high, it's not possible to get to the summit by car and we didn't have time to climb the summit by foot. It stank of sulphur and the air felt peculiarly warm. It was deserted and the skies were solid. Roads were strewn with black rocks and dust. "Chiuso!", said the locals. Closed. An eruption was happening. I did not want to die in a stream of molten lava and drove accordingly. The Fiat 500 has crap brakes, no power and seems to ride 6" higher than any other small hatchback should, but it went quicker than any Targa Florio racer has ever done, I'm sure.

We had returned the car, quite battered after it's hot lap the day before, and spent hours waiting for flights to resume before being bussed elsewhere for a different flight altogether. Back at Gatwick in the small hours, we had missed the last train back home, as well as the last bus, and no one would rent us a car for some reason. You don't get this on a trackday.

Knackered Jag to Valhalla

Car;   eBay-bought 1996 Jaguar XJ6. Better than
                 a Boeing 737.

Location;   From England to Norway.

Duration;   Three days.

15000 kroner sounds like a lot of money. And it is. Roughly 1500 British pounds is what the Jaguar dealer in Oslo wanted to supply an air conditioning pump for a 1996 Jaguar XJ6. Fifteen hundred quid. And that price excluded fitting. "British cårs åre sø unræliable", said the man behind the counter. This wasn't my car, nor my problem, but things *are* expensive in Norway. Obscene prices, dreadful beer, an unhealthy obsession with the great outdoors and people with splendid cheekbones are what we Brits know Norway for. But mainly the prices. A medium pizza in a high street place; £25. A pint of Speckled Hen; £12. Meat? I'm surprised they haven't turned to cannibalism. And when a mate mentioned the main dealer wanted *one and a half thousand pounds* for a poxy little component, I was appalled, but not surprised.

There are many chapters in this book extolling the virtues of budget airline travel, but I hate Ryanair. I hate the smug arsehole who runs it, Michael O'Leary (uncle of TV presenter Demot). For years, he traded on "yeah we're shit but we're cheap so get lost if you don't like it". No one is obliged to use them, but I resented the attitude, the crushingly poor customer service and the sheer *misery* of the airline. Other budget airlines were probably as equally set up to provide a miserable bus service with wings, but O'Leary's inane face really riles me. He owns a taxi company, in Dublin, with one car. His car, only for him. He pays all the taxi fees so that he can use the taxi lanes. Perfectly legal and, had it been someone else, a bit of legal chicanery I would have grudgingly admired. But I hate him. Got a complaint? There was a time when you could only complain by fax. Who owns a bloody fax machine?! And on calling to see why your fax isn't answered, you got a woman in Hungary who really, really did not give a shit. "So vot? Vot yo gonna do?", I was told, on the only occasion I managed to get through to them by phone, before they hung up. They've made a genuine effort to go upmarket lately, but I still make every effort to avoid them. Priority queue? I'm paying more to receive only slightly less bad customer service because you don't employ sufficient people to handle your customers? Sod off. I'd like to piss on O'Leary's shoes, and tell him he can pay a tenner for me not to give him a full bladder's worth on his Brogues. So, I have a mate in need of a car part, a chance to avoid Ryanair and am the kind of chap who will find any excuse for a road trip. When a meeting in Oslo came up, the plan was practically written for me. I was not off to Stansted airport. I was off to Grantham, Lincolnshire.

Jaguar owners are lovely sorts, in my experience. When I placed a wanted ad for a very specific XJ6, with a budget of £1500, I hoped for some lovely old stick who had given up driving and wanted their car to go to a good home. I didn't admit that the car would be on a one-way trip to Valhalla, to be butchered for the only one working part I insisted on; an air con pump. But so many are snotters at this price. I looked at a fair few, all with buggered suspension bushes, wretched interiors, drooping headlinings and gearbox lurchiness. I could live with this, but it had to get me to Norway reliably. In winter. Cars that looked great in adverts were sold by aggressive gypsies, traders with no paperwork masquerading as private sellers and, in the case of a car I travelled all the way to sodding Croydon to see, a homeless person who was living in the car. The answer lay in Grantham. A pirate radio DJ who always wanted a Jaguar, and then wanted rid of it for reasons I don't remember, had the right year, spec and paperwork for a car that looked half-right and only shook slightly violently at speeds over 50 mph. It was snowing. We wouldn't be going that quick. Sold to the man with a plan to avoid Ryanair. Dayinsure.com covered it and I rounded up the lads. I'm not stupid enough to attempt this trip alone.

There is a ferry crossing to Norway. It's a freight-only thing and runs a triangular route from Immingham to Gothenburg in Sweden, then Larvik in Norway before heading south-west back to the UK. It's not cheap and takes forever. Sir William Lyons, of Jaguar, said his cars should have "grace, pace and space" and, on that basis, they make perfect continental transport. We would do the minimum of travel at sea, Eurotunnelling to France, up through the low countries, overnighting in Germany, up through Denmark before catching the Color Line ferry from the top of Denmark to the bottom of Norway and then a run up the E18 motorway to Oslo. As a bonus bit of smuggling, I packed the boot with low-cost beer and a few bottles of port. Four up, we gently drove down to Folkestone. I was behaving because, at this point, the car was registered to me. In Dover, knowing the XJ6 would not be coming back, I completed the bit of the V5 log book that says 'permanently exported' and listed the new owner as 'Mr. John Three Jags Prescott', Hull, England, then posted it first class to the DVLA.

We boarded the Eurotunnel, me, Gay Luke, Tipex and Daz, in good spirits. The Jag had a cassette deck and we had each brought along a tape from our youth. I had some Japanese techno, which was thrown out of the window the first time my back was turned. Gay Luke (who is, despite his nom de guerre, mostly heterosexual) had brought a tape of his own band, playing their own tunes, which no one wants to hear. Tipex had brought MC Hammer. Everyone loves Hammer. The tape went in and got stuck in. We were stuck with either no music or MC Hammer, for the whole journey. You can't touch this. Literally. The car was (and it seems sad talking about it in the past tense) a 1996 Jaguar XJ6 of the type X300. The model (and it's similar sibling the X308) benefited from all the Ford QA work of the early '90s and yet retained the Jaggyness lacking in the X350 that came later. They had spent £200 million on robots and stuff, the Queen visited the factory and bought one, and even today they seem as undervalued in the UK as beer is overvalued in Norway. Jaguar had lived in the shadow of British Leyland for so long that their cars had a poor reputation. But the XJ6, y'know—it's bloody good. This last sentence perhaps explains why I am not a particularly successful motoring journalist.

As we shimmied across grey European motorways, we had the chance to reflect on what was, for £1500, a very cheap luxury car. It shimmied because the suspension was shagged out. A common complaint, as British roads are so speed-bumped, traffic-calmed, potholed and horrible that these things wear out prematurely. Jaguars (hot XJR aside) ride so nicely and it's a pity that, as these cars fall into the bangernomics category of ownership, they don't fix these things. The car weight, unladen, 1800 kg. All up, wet, with a glovebox full to capacity with Werther's Original, we must have been half a tonne more. 0–60 mph is about 8.5 seconds with a top whack of 135 mph, which is what we aimed for as we crossed the border into Germany. The last time something from Browns Lane crossed the Ruhr valley at this speed, it was being pursued by Messerschmitts. The shimmying stopped over 90 mph, the weather went from gentle snowflake to proper gusts of white stuff and it got dark.

I had brought along the lads because I wanted to share the driving in such conditions. We were on Chinese tyres. By law in Germany, and elsewhere in Northern Europe, you must use winter tyres. We Brits don't bother. Our car had two Dunlops on the back for pushing and two mismatched Chinese things on the front. The Dunlops were so old they were probably made at Fort Dunlop in Birmingham, iconic industrial building turned Travelodge (like much of the industry in the West Midlands, it seems). Fort Dunlop was once the world's biggest single factory, employing 3200 people in one single building and 10000 on site. It was built in 1916 and, when the production of tyres there had ended, surveyors found that the building's frame was so well built that it had only moved 2 mm in a century. Sorry, I've been driving for hours without sleep; I'm prone to wandering off on architectural tangents. We dumped the Jag in a blizzard and checked into a hotel. We then got a little tiddly on Weißbeer with schnapps chasers, ate sausage, potatoes and sauerkraut, and fell asleep.

The morning brought a whiteout. My ~~ballast~~ passengers sat in the car eating mints and dancing to MC Hammer, while I used my bank card and fingernails to scrape the ice off the windscreen. They really were useless cretins, the lot of them. Gay Luke didn't want to get any more snow on his pointy shoes, Daz was still drunk and Tipex wound his window down to helpfully point out that we had parked in/on a bicycle rack. I continued to scrape snow and ice off until I found a parking ticket and binned it, hoping Prescott would cop for it. Actually, I rather like him. He's a Jag man with four speeding convictions who was the only guest on Top Gear to ever get Clarkson to shut up.

The car was not moving. Passengers helpfully bounced up and down in their seats to Hammertime and we got moving. The XJ6 has such a long wheelbase that we zig-zagged with ease up the main street in a long, lazy fishtailing motion. The tyres were crap but only needed to last two more countries. Into Denmark and the snow covered the motorway, leaving two strips of clear tarmac a few inches wide. These narrowed and narrowed, until the last bit of grip we had was left behind. North, onwards, in the blinding snow. The motorway was down to one lane due to an accident, cops too busy with wreckage to look twice at our tired old car shimmying by.

I don't know what the laws are for driving in Denmark, but by now it didn't matter, we were knackered and just wanted it over. Daz needed a poo. It's pathetic, a man of his age, whining for a poo like a schoolboy, but he'd overdone the sauerkraut and was insistent we stopped. We did. Then had to drive quicker to make up for lost time in worsening conditions, swapping drivers to stay fresh. We had a ferry to catch and were chronically behind schedule. "No good", he said, face bathed in sweat, "we have to stop again". And again. Driving on snow was manageable but the stopping and starting was tricky. We slithered into Hirtshals, having missed our ferry, but able to catch the next. As we boarded, Daz dashed for the toilet. I told him we were not stopping again and waved the snowy port goodbye. Hirtshals is an anagram of last shit. Oh the irony.

Smuggling is big business in Norway. They're not in the EU and have lots of people travelling to Denmark and elsewhere to buy alcohol and cigarettes and other stuff on the cheap. Customs stop lots of cars and check all the paperwork. I know I am on illegal tyres, iffy insurance and (I am not proud of this) perhaps still just a little bit hazy from the night before. Drink driving, if you didn't know, is punishable by a proper jail sentence here. I follow a Polish-registered E-class Mercedes down the unloading ramp, not wanting to stop as I doubt we'd get moving again. The snow is a good 6" deep here, or more. I have to stop for the police. Window down. He speaks perfect English (of course) and looks suspicious; "Ah, nice Jaguar—isn't this John Prescott's car?" A ripple of fear courses through me before he explains; "Top Gear, two Jags, very funny!" He waves us on. Everyone loves old Jaguars.

The sea here is frozen solid. Everything is monochrome. The snow has that beautiful dusty, sparkly effect that we never seem to get in England. It's dry, cold and beautiful, and we are stuck, fast. The E18 motorway is but a kilometre or so away from the port, but the old cat is going nowhere. We drink the contents of the boot (unchecked by the friendly policeman but in clear view of his warm little hut), beer first, then port. My mate turns up with a trailer and some tools and saves us. One air con pump with a free Jaguar, delivered. He coughs up 15000 kroner for the car, plus some cash to cover our travel expenses and we go to the pub to spend it all on obscenely priced beer and talk up our winter driving skills. Tomorrow, I have a meeting and avoided one Ryanair flight to get here, a result.

The Jaguar collected a huge amount of parking tickets and set off a few speed cameras in and around Oslo before being broken for spares. If driving agencies around Europe ever pool their data, then Three Jags Prescott is in big trouble.

The cost of spares is so high here that the Jag paid for itself many times over and my mate had as much fun before chopping it up as we had on our road trip getting here. It was sad to kill it, but I like to think we took it on a journey to Valhalla, the enormous heavenly hall where slain heroes go, ruled over by Odin, piloted on the journey there by the Valkyries. Or in our case, four haggard Brits. And as for 'unreliable' British cars, when the broken air con pump was finally stripped out, the original factory sticker on it said Nippon Denso. Made in Japan.

Autobahn V(olvo)max

Car;   Rented Volvo V70 D5. Etch-a-sketch five-
                banger tank.

Location;   A8 Autobahn, Stuttgart to Ulm, Germany.

Duration;   Half a day.

I have always had a soft spot for Volvos. I once owned a
TWR-tuned 850, a model made famous for entering the
British Touring Car Championship in the 1990s. It is a boxy
estate car with terrible aerodynamics, which Volvo solved
by just adding more and more power to simply push the
air out of the way. Brute force over science. I heard that
the works Volvo team once put a taxidermied Labrador in
the boot of the 850 estate, strapped it down and charged
around for a few laps of Silverstone for a laugh. It was a
winning car though. A marque once known for its safety
features and staid image, now putting in thumping wins
on track. As with many of these 'Nothing handles like a
rental' trips, there is no guarantee of what you'll be given
on collection, but on arriving with the singular intention
of vmaxing a car on the autobahn, a Volvo seemed
strangely appropriate. I didn't have a taxidermied
passenger. I had my mate, Graham, who turned out to be
less use than a stuffed dog.

Graham is a Brit who lives in China. The thing with China
is that it's nigh on impossible for westerners to legally
drive there. China's roads are crowded bedlam, and as
Graham had not driven for so long, the prospect of miles
of clear autobahn seemed strange to him. All I needed
was his eyes to help spot any potential disaster. The Volvo
V70 has a notional top speed of 210 kph. At such a speed,
you are covering nearly 6 metres a second. That's like

driving from London to Sheffield in an hour, something you could have attempted legally in 1965 before motorway speed limits were imposed in the UK. Germany, although increasingly restricting the amount of derestricted autobahns, still has large swathes of road where the top speed is up to you. And your spotter, who, in my case, was both hungover and jetlagged.

Not all autobahns are derestricted. And of those that are, some suffer from such heavy traffic that a proper vmax attempt is impossible. If it rains (*bei Nässe* in German), you are obliged to slow down. There are various websites that will help you pick the right spot. I have no connection with it, but www.autobahn-speedhunter.com looks like an interesting place to start. In my case, I chose the A8 that runs from Stuttgart to Ulm because, at the southern end, it is both derestricted and rather scenic. It is quite twisty though. A gentle curve at, say, 60 mph seemingly becomes a hairpin at twice the speed. Volvos, as much as I love 'em, aren't famed for their high-speed handling and I am no Rickard Rydell. I know all this now, and you'll know that I didn't die during my vmax attempt as I'm writing this, but it had the potential for high-speed disaster. Graham's job was to spot the potential disaster, but he was fighting jetlag with miniatures of airline whisky.

Getting up to 150 kph is pretty easy. Thereafter, the five-pot engine starts to run out of puff and the 'squarodynamics' of the Volvo hold it back. The required driving technique was similar to that of something like an old Beetle or 2CV; you have no surplus power so are loathe to lift for anything. Scrubbing off 10 kph when you're nearly flat out means that you'll need many kilometres to regain it, acceleration at the top of a rented

Volvo's gearbox being scant. At 150 kph, Graham was drunk and scared. "This is fun!", he clearly lied, fumbling for the cap on his miniature that had fallen in that black hole which all modern cars seem to have, between the seat and centre console near the seatbelt point. He gave up looking and just finished the bottle. 160 kph. He decided to fetch another bottle but there was no way I was stopping, so he unbuckled and leant over to the back seats where he had more in his bag, sticking his sizeable arse in my face. My shouting startled him and his scream startled me. He went face-first into the back before reappearing, red-faced, with two more miniatures. No, I didn't fancy a drink. 170 kph. He carefully climbed into the front and I reminded him to buckle up.

I was once contacted by a TV company who was looking for someone to participate in a programme about motoring. Basically, they wanted someone to say that motorways in the UK should be derestricted, like Germany. I resent having words put in my mouth and put some words in their ear. I didn't participate in the programme. Derestricted roads only work in Germany because of the conditions unique to the topography and their road network. I guess we can thank Hitler and Speer for that. The line of sight is huge, sometimes maybe 5–10 km, and there are far fewer exits meaning fewer lane changes and this, coupled with (generally) better driver discipline, means that there are places where you can safely travel at very high speeds for long distances. I was trying to explain this to calm Graham's nerves but he wasn't well. He had gone a sort of parchment colour.

At 195 kph, I thought the Volvo was about flat out. Then a bit of a plain. The needle crept up to 198 kph and stayed there. I didn't mind not hitting the 210 kph maximum quoted speed of the car, but falling short of the double tonne was annoying. 199 kph. "GOOOO-AAAAAN", shouted Graham, which I took as encouragement, but was actually the sound of him expelling a huge burp with an unmistakable smoky, peaty aroma. Famous Grouse was my guess. "No", said Graham, "Baijiu". Chinese whisky. At this point, he decided to put the radio on.

Regular visitors to Deutschland will know that, if you switch the radio on, there is a very high risk of David Hasselhoff being played. I explained this to Graham and, as God is my witness (thankfully, there were no palpable witnesses to our behaviour), the words of the 'hof burst forth from the speakers; "*I've bin lookin' for freeeedom*". This caused much hilarity, so much so that I hadn't noticed the 911 sat a few mm off our rear bumper flashing it's lights. It does not matter how fast you go on the autobahn, there will always be someone faster. Still, at 199 kph, I moved over, but didn't move my right foot off the gas. We had come a long way and I really wanted to hit the double tonne.

Many autobahns have only two lanes. This means you need to look a long way down the road to spot Russian truckers who will pull out without even breaking the steady rhythm of their masturbating, let alone use their mirrors to spot two laughing Englishmen in a 199-kph Volvo. I had to hit 200 kph. Igor was out and in (and probably spent) just before we arse-ended him. 199 kph. Graham finally realised the importance of this last 1 kph. We stared at the speedo, the engine howled and the wind rushed against us. Graham, many years ago, back in England, used to own a Lotus. He necked another miniature and looked contemplative. We had a Colin Chapman moment and pulled over into a service station. Let's simplicate and add lightness.

While Graham went for a wee, I emptied out all the rubbish. The 1600-kg Volvo was about 1 kg lighter. I needed to save more weight. I threw out Graham's coat as it was soaked in whisky anyway. As I was doing this, I looked on in horror as Graham returned and ripped off a windscreen wiper and threw it in some bushes. It was like watching a playful but savage dog chew up your furniture. As I was rummaging in the bushes to retrieve the wiper, I noticed him in the boot. Out came the spare wheel and he rolled it down the car park. It was steep enough to gain sufficient speed to outrun me and came to rest against an Opel, which, in my paranoia, I took to be an unmarked police car, so I left it there in case someone spotted us. I turned around to head back to the car to see Graham wrenching off the other wiper. We got back in the car. I confiscated his final miniature of whisky. We must have improved aerodynamics and lost sufficient weight to hit 200 kph now, surely?

It was getting dark and a bit cloudy, and the afternoon's commuters were starting to join the autobahn. 100, 150, 180 kph all come fairly easily. "I need a drink", said Graham. I had to focus. 185, 190, 195 kph and then the glacial movement of the speedo for the final climb to 199 kph. The needle crept towards the summit slower than a Sherpa with altitude sickness. And there it sat. 199 kph for mile after mile. It felt like a failure. "I need a drink", said Graham. I took his miniature, put the window down and lobbed it out. We argued for a bit, then put the radio on to break the awkward silence. "*Alle die hits mit Radio Bayern—und jetzt—David Hasselhoff!*" I looked at the speedo. 200 magnificent kph! Back at Stuttgart airport, Graham blamed the wiper theft on squirrels and I blamed everything on him. The insurance excess waiver covered the wipers but I got invoiced for the missing spare wheel. I didn't care. I had achieved a 'hof-assisted 200 kph. I haven't seen Graham since.

The man who never was—in a Vanquish

Car;   Press fleet-supplied Aston Martin
                 Vanquish Volante. The name's Duisberg,
                 Rich Duisberg, and I feel like a berk.

Location;   London and Chatham, England.

Duration;   Two nights.

It started with a trip to a junkyard in Lincolnshire which
had hundreds and hundreds of broken shop dummies.
£20 bought me one with roughly the right amount of
limbs and the head on the right way. This was to be the
body of Glyndwr Michael, a Welsh vagrant who died in
1943 after eating rat poison. Shop dummies are strangely
inflexible, so I unscrewed him at the waist, sat his top half
in the passenger seat of my old Porsche and put his legs in
the back, and drove (causing much rubbernecking on the
A1) to London, where the story gets even stranger.

After having made a few low-budget films with the guys at CBS's XCAR, I had pitched the idea of a bigger film about an Aston Martin racing driver I had long admired, a chap called Jock Horsfall. I expected the chances of Aston Martin agreeing to give me a car were slim to none, yet my scrounging emails must have hit the right inbox, i.e. someone who knew who Horsfall was, because here I was in London with a cameraman and a dismembered shop dummy in an underground car park looking for 'my' Vanquish. I had arranged a nighttime shoot to tell the story of one of Horsfall's greatest feats—his participation in the Second World War's Operation Mincemeat. I found the Vanquish and, awestruck, started it. The naturally aspirated V12 in an underground car park sounded like the blitz. But the electronic handbrake was stuck on. What's that about first impressions? We sat there trying to work out what to do next.

Jock raced Aston Martins in the 1930s. He was quick but famously gung-ho. He was also a great practical joker, wiring up toilet seats to car batteries and writing mucky ditties about girlfriends. In the war, he worked for British military intelligence alongside Bond creator, Ian Fleming. It is said that Jock was the inspiration for Bond; he was a real character. The purpose of my film was to use the Vanquish as a backdrop to tell the story of his life and, in particular, his participation in one of the most outrageous military operations of all time, Operation Mincemeat, which was also the inspiration for the war film "The Man Who Never Was". Bear with me; I'll get to the car shortly because, while the big Aston was a disappointment, this story is amazing.

Jock was part of a team including Ian Fleming and worked alongside espionage experts with the most English of names, Cholmondeley and Montagu. Their group was known as the double X committee, double X standing for double cross. Montagu's brother was spying for the Russians, but if I get any deeper into the fascinating intrigue of this bunch, we won't get anywhere near the car stuff. Their plan was to plant fake invasion plans into the hands of the Nazis in order to have them divert their troops and resources. They planned on taking a corpse, dressing him as a British Officer, planting false information on it and leaving the body where the Nazis would find it.

I tried to explain what I was doing to an inquisitive policeman, but it must have sounded like I was on acid. I was relieved when he didn't look in the boot of the Vanquish. It was 2 am and we were filming the introduction to this incredible story outside the building where it all started, Hackney Mortuary. He left us alone.

Jock and co stole the body of Glyndwr Michael, a man with no next of kin, and dressed him as Major Martin, compete with a briefcase full of 'secrets'. We made do with my shop dummy dressed in the uniform I wear to the Goodwood Revival on occasion, in half, in the boot. We drove around the streets of London, telling the story. Jock used a Ford van to shift the corpse, but there was no way I was driving a Tranny when there was an Aston Martin available. The electronic parking brake had fixed itself, at last, and while Jock drove flat out overnight to Scotland before the body decomposed further, we drove around London while late-night boozers called us rude names.

I felt very self-conscious driving this car. As the Volante (convertible) and filming with the roof down, with a lighting rig in my face and cameras set up, I must have looked ridiculous. "Try harder, lads", was one memorable shout. I suspect it's a British thing; anyone enjoying such an opulent bit of machinery in public seems fair game. I did feel like a berk.

Jock arrived in a Scottish shipyard, surprisingly on time and in one piece after having driven clean over a traffic island in central London and nearly hitting a tram shelter. Did I mention he had to wear special glasses, as he was nearly blind? Jock posed with the canister containing the body before offloading it to a waiting submarine, taking a selfie while sipping a celebratory cup of tea (see pic). There's an anecdote which suggests that the body was so rotten on arrival that they had to hurriedly find another and used a body washed up on a beach from the aircraft carrier HMS Dasher, which exploded and sank near Glasgow around the time Jock arrived. Had my own corpse 'gone off', I would have been happy to mow down one of the mouthy street drunks who had so vocally disapproved of my choice of car and use theirs instead.

We thumped down the motorway to Chatham's historic dockyard, where I had negotiated the use of our own submarine, albeit as a backdrop. I am an ordinary sort of chap. I have three children, like to grow tomatoes and follow the Leicester Tigers rugby team. Sometimes, on Sundays, I like to play Scrabble. Yet, here I was, in a car worth more than what I paid for my house, skulking about in a dark shipyard telling tales of wartime espionage. Sometimes, I have to pinch myself. Telling the tale, in such a prestigious car, in such interesting locations, it's hard not to feel like you are a tiny bit of the action somehow. It's not the car alone that does it, but telling the tale as you drive against such an evocative backdrop somehow gets under your skin.

The body was delivered by submarine and washed up on a Spanish beach where, as planned, it ended up in the hands of the Nazis, who bought the deception and moved their troops, allowing the Allies to invade Sicily with considerably less opposition. But Jock's adventures were not over. He broke his neck twice in other wartime adventures and, when hostilities ended, went back to racing, before coming a cropper for a final, fatal time at Silverstone in 1949 in a near-undriveable ERA. Today, there's an annual Aston Martin race in his name, the St John Horsfall Trophy.

The Aston had a few electrical glitches, a horrible CVT-alike slushbox and was so big I kerbed a wheel or two in central London. Filming one sequence in the pitch black, the cameraman stood deep in a cornfield, waiting for me to drive by. All the talk of decomposing bodies in the dark must have played with his mind, as he stepped back and trod on a rotting scarecrow's head. I heard his scream over the V12 and laughed nearly as loud. That was perhaps the most fun I had behind the wheel of the Vanquish.

I wrapped up filming and went to the pub, buying my 'corpse' a pint and bag of cheese and onion crisps, amusing/confusing fellow drinkers. A tiny bit of me likes to think that Jock would have approved. I took the uniform off it and went home, *sans* Aston, second class. My 'man who never was' now lives in an office in London, naked.

Joop's greenhouse

Car;   Can't remember mine, can't list all of his.

Location;   A greenhouse, the Netherlands.

Duration;   One very full day.

One of the most common motoring subjects on the Internet, apart from "Help, my Peugeot is knackered", is the classic 'Dream car lineup' thread where people list theoretical collections of motors they'll almost certainly never own. My own list, even whittled to a bare minimum, has 12 cars. I once met a chap who actually bought everything on *his* list. All 650 of them. Six hundred and fifty. This is not the story of some Arab's oil-money-funded collection in a sterile showroom but that of a modest farmer from Holland, Joop Stolze, a man (and private collection) I came across totally by chance.

I had been writing content for a book called "1001 Dream Cars You Must Drive Before You Die", which can still sometimes be found in the bargain bin of bookshops. The book has about a dozen contributors, of which I was one, each with their own area of expertise. I just got excited and picked all the things that interested me, such as '70s Alpinas and '60s Maseratis. I had never contributed to a book before. It's bloody hard work (my coal-mining granddad might disagree, were he still alive). Writing in a set format about cars I like the look of but know nothing about was asking for trouble; there's only so many times you can lift things off Wikipedia before the reader nods off and before the publisher gets wind. I found writing in a very tightly defined style a slog, as was being obliged to use American English to satisfy the publisher. Aluminium, colour, bonnet, fag—*there*. This is my book with my language; if you don't like it—stick it up your arse. Anyway, on the long list of cars I was claiming to be an expert on was the Maserati Mistral. When you're bored of reading this, have a Google of the Mistral. You'll find that there's feck all info of interest about it anywhere. I knew the Mistral was named after a wind, but that left me a few hundred words short. I was desperate for info. When I saw a Mistral for sale, in the Netherlands, I decided to call the seller to see what I could learn.

I now know that Joop made his money by growing orchids, a seasonal trade, and that during quiet months, he bought and rallied a Triumph TR3 and, slowly, his collection grew, and included a Mistral. Although he now has a tidy showroom, with a shiny Ferrari 512 and some fine classic motorbikes, until a couple of years ago, it was a completely different set-up. I asked him if I could see the car as I was passing on business, making it plain that I wasn't coming to buy, just to learn what I could. He was understandably grumpy and was probably telling me to get stuffed, only in Dutch, but as I didn't speak Dutch, I couldn't be entirely sure what he was on about and understood that he was inviting me over for pancakes and Maserati chat because that's what I wanted to hear. I am so glad I did gate-crash, because it was spectacular.

I have been asked to name the location many times, but promised Joop I never would. He has since moved to bigger, professional premises and you'll find him quick enough if you look, but back then, his colossal horde was private and located in his old orchid greenhouses, at the end of a lane, down a dyke in the Netherlands. His house was a modest little dormer bungalow with small rooms and big windows, maybe two bedrooms and a pretty garden. Behind it was a wooden workshop, which served as a kind of porch to slightly run down whitewashed greenhouses. In front of this workshop were a dozen classic cars, some stacked on top of one another, but all fascinating. A saggy looking Maserati, a badly painted Mustang and others. He came out of the house and he looked me up and down, decided that I wasn't going to steal anything and left me to it. In the doorway of the workshop was a younger guy who spoke good English. He had an E-Type in half and was rewiring it. We said hello. "If you like those…", he said in the direction of the cars outside that clearly had me interested, and then just nodded at a wooden door off the back of the porch which led to the greenhouses behind.

The huge heated greenhouse where Joop originally grew orchids was crammed with his colossal dream car lineup in various states of repair. Since starting his collection c.30 years ago, he had accumulated many extremely rare or unique vehicles, and at the same time, people had started to find him and buy some of his surplus, hence the little workshop on the front. Cars only got restored when they really needed it. The condition of the cars in the greenhouse would, by a trader, be described as 'honest'. A detailer would have a dicky fit.

The patina of ancient paintwork, tears in leather, rust and cobwebs show the cars as they were last enjoyed. Some, without doubt, would have wallet-raped many of their previous owners. Others, like a pair of pristine Porsche Speedsters, looked just like they've left the factory. I was completely stunned and you'll have to excuse the terrible pics, I only had a cheapo camera, being prepared only for a Mistral, not hundreds of cars. The conditions were humid, as you'd expect, although the roof kept the rain off. Some of the rot was spectacular. Thick, old paint holding together the scabrous panels beneath. Doors and bodies that iron oxide was gently, but inevitably, forcing in different directions. Lush plants grew and tyres silently leaked and cracked. It was a strange but beautiful sight, lichen living on a yellow Elan, nature overtaking everything.

There was a definite theme to his collection. Most cars were from 1930 to 1970 and he clearly had a passion for coupes, Italian beauties and classic British stuff. There were groups of very similar cars, a line of TR3s, many MGs, a batch of Porsche 914s. Amongst the visual chaos and decay, there was a rough organisation along marque/country lines. Certain marques were almost over-represented (how many 911s does one man need?), yet others conspicuous by their absence. A BMW Z1 looked lonely, for example. There were just two Lotuses (note, only onanists say Lotii), yet nearly every variation of 1950s and 60s Alfa Romeo I could think of. Aside from a couple of Z cars, there was nothing Japanese. As a fan of 60s and 70s exotica, I was stiffer than a used paintbrush at Joop's collection of Maseratis; *another* Mistral, a Bora, an Indy, Meraks (note, plural), Ghibli and Quattroporte. Autobianchi? Over there. Cisitalia? Behind that Mercedes. He must have spotted I had wandered off and came to catch me trespassing. I don't think he was concerned about me stealing or damaging anything, more that he was perhaps embarrassed at the state of the place. It was hard for me to make him understand, but I *love* this stuff. I love the last signs of life in cars that can only have been owned by interesting people. The scratches tell a story. Bonnets up. What was it that killed this car? He relaxed. A bit.

I asked Joop about his horde; "I don't like obvious questions", he said. I asked him how long it would take to remove a car from the very middle of the greenhouse. "Yes. Questions like that". It was a bit awkward. The collection gets shuffled once a week, he said. He has two guys in his workshop restoring cars I couldn't identify, let alone rewire. Impressive stuff. Facels and Comètes, brands long-swallowed by bigger companies, Jaguars, Lancias, Pontiacs and Packards all stacked under whitewashed glass ready for resurrection. Cars with faded notes left to future owners explaining how to operate things, cars with radios left tuned into long-gone LW stations, cars with bags of vital bits in the footwell. The history here was immense. Plastic buttons had decayed and looked like sugar cubes. A cat lived in a Packard. These were, in many cases, some of the last examples of marques made half a century ago. Models that even Wikipedia does not know. I asked Joop if he had an actual list of this lot. "Ja. In my head". His knowledge was immense; quantities made, values, common problems on uncommon cars. He worked from 7 am to midnight, every night and told me he once spent five years chasing a single car just because he wanted it. He still found time to drive them though and had restored certain cars just to enter specific events, classic rallies in Triumphs and Jaguars, for example. It was time to leave.

All of it was beautiful and more than a little melancholy. In all the excitement, I forgot to ask about the Mistral, but can tell you that the washer bottle is a plastic bag. The resultant book was dull beyond words. I recall the only thing of interest I sneaked past the publisher was a snippet in my bio, inside the jacket. I claimed to be the personal fitness guru to rubbish Ferrari F1 driver, Luca Badoer. Those who know me will be aware that I have successfully avoided any form of PE since leaving school. Maybe if enough people buy that rubbish book, I'll earn enough to turn my dream car list into reality and track down a working Mistral somewhere.

Car launch fun and why you should never trust a review

Car;   Toyota C-HR. You will never trust a
              motoring review ever again.

Location;   Madrid and Jarama, Spain.

Duration;   24 hours.

You'll probably know PistonHeads. It's a forum rather like
Mumsnet, but instead of being about mums mostly
bitching about useless husbands, it's about blokes mostly
bitching about people bumming their dog. There's
sometimes some car natter on there, which I enjoy. A
forum user called 'hidetheelephants', impressed by my
automotive adventures to date, sort of challenged me to
see if I could get invited on a new car launch. I might not
be a big fan of many new cars but I do like a challenge. I
had written a favourable review about a Lexus and,
perhaps with that in mind, I managed to get hold of the
right person in Toyota's press office. After some email
ping pong, I managed to get an invitation to the launch of
the Toyota C-HR. This is the very latest, high-tech, funky
looking hybrid. The kind of car I normally have no interest
in whatsoever. It gave me the opportunity to see how the
media really works, to mix with proper journos and to be
one of the first people in Europe to drive a brand new
model. Also, and for this reason I'll never trust another
car review in my life, it meant a private jet flight to a five-
star resort in Madrid where the launch would be held.

A mate of mine in publishing once warned me about 'car
people'. Men who seem to live for nothing else, obsess
over cars and are seemingly incapable of showing an
interest for anything else in life. These men are usually
single. They move from press launch to press launch, are

paid a pittance and will talk loudly about the time they beat Dave from Scottish SUV Owners Magazine to the keys of the first Renault Felcher in the UK. These men can be spotted at social events from quite a distance, as they invariably do air-steering as they tell yet another amusing anecdote. I would really rather not mix with such people. Maybe I am one of them myself. Places were strictly limited and these 'car people' were expected to write their own copy and take their own pics. No one brought a sidekick. I would expect that most would use Toyota's own press photography (helpfully provided on a quality, branded USB stick). None of them would say a bad word. They all wanted to be invited on the next gig, and the one after that, in an endless loop of nice nosh and foreign travel. This is not my style.

I asked, if possible, if I could bring a 'cracking new photographer' along with me. There was more email ping pong and, eventually, I got a yes. On new car launches, I believe, it is common for these single journos to be paired up. I'm pretty sure no one would want to be stuck with me and I'd rather be travelling with my girlfriend. She had picked up a camera bag off Gumtree, packed it with rubble and checked it in at Farnborough Airport. She was my 'photographer'. If anyone realised we were a couple, both of us would have been chucked off the trip. Farnborough Airport is the nicest, most professional and relaxing place I have ever travelled from.

We queued separately, checked in separately and then co-incidentally sat together on the Boeing 737 that seated 60 selected motoring journalists, plus me and my girlfriend. "I'm terrified of flying", she admitted and made best use of the complimentary in-flight service. Bacardi and Cokes, by the double, served at 15-min intervals for the duration of the flight. The meal was splendid and there was legroom to accommodate a giraffe.

On landing, we were whisked to a small, quiet terminal, had our bags packed onto the bus and taken to a beautiful villa, where we enjoyed a delicious tapas buffet and were given the keys to our cars. There was a large map with the test route explained to us. The sat nav was pre-programmed with the same route. We were to take this route. We were not to deviate from this route. This is the test route. Bollocks to that.

North of Madrid is Jarama, home of the Spanish Grand Prix between 1968 and 1981, when it was deemed too tight for modern racing. In the final race here, Gilles Villeneuve's Ferrari had the entire pack all over him but unable to overtake due to his canny defensive driving and the lack of overtaking places. It was the final win of his career and so close that the first five cars crossed the line just 1.24 seconds apart. We peeled off from the convoy and zipped along to Jarama. Security were surprised to see a pretty blonde and slightly squiffy 'photographer' driven by a shambolic Englishman in a car no one had seen before on Belgian trade plates. We were waved in. I'm not saying what we got up to other than to say we were photographed snogging on the top step of the podium afterwards. We then had to drive like the clappers to reach the official stop where we were glared at for obviously having taken the piss.

More driving in the afternoon (official route this time) took us to a five-star hotel in central Madrid, a place of traffic chaos, unrelentingly rude drivers and armed police. I was tired of one-way systems and bus lanes. The title of this book might be 'Nothing handles like a rental car', but a press car runs it a close second. The hotel was opulent. We checked in. We were grilled. My 'photographer' batted away photography questions fired by Keith from Caravan Towcar monthly. Technical questions were answered with airy-fairy arty nonsense such as "never mind that, isn't the light *marvellous* here?!" There were two bottles of complimentary champagne, an exquisite dinner and any thoughts of saying anything unkind about the Toyota Whatever-it-is evaporated. There was a presentation about the chassis engineering which I found genuinely interesting, but no one listened. The complimentary bar was opening.

There's a very strong bond between the press and car manufacturers. They need each other. As magazine sales are in decline, they need advertising revenue more than ever. This usually means the car manufacturers. These manufacturers often cling to the theory that people still buy and read magazines when considering buying a car. Most mags have an online version, as an afterthought, which you either have to pay to read or is rammed with adverts—but nearly no one pays for digital content. There's an unwritten rule that, if something is on the Internet, it should be free to read (regardless of what it costs to produce). Quality, critical content costs money to produce and, so, as this situation exists where the press and manufacturers are locked together, hardly anyone says anything bad about anything. For example, I was once in a What Car? sort of magazine as a reader, invited to the unveiling of the MG6, at Longbridge, and invited to give my feedback. We were asked to rate it from one star to five for certain categories. I gave it one star with some honest feedback. When I bought a copy of the magazine, I found a picture of myself with quotes saying how much I liked it and how good the seats were, and not a one- but a four-star rating. The MG6 was utter dog muck.

You can find reviews of Toyota's C-HR all over the place. Some will have been written by the same journos who attended this trip. Some of these reviews will be accurate and honest. Some will have been written by people addled by incredibly generous hospitality looking for the next jolly. One will have been written by somebody winging it with his girlfriend and accompanied by some slightly iPhoney photographs. Never mind the ISO setting, the ambience was *wonderful*. Read it or leave it, but never buy a car on a journalist's say-so.

Senna's Merscabies at the Nürburgring GP circuit

Car;   A scrounged Mercedes-Benz 190E 2.3 16V
                Cosworth.

Location;   The Nürburgring GP circuit, Germany.

Duration;   24 hours over there, plus 8 hours drive
                each way there and back.

I love following in the footsteps of my heroes. Usually, it's
in machinery totally unrelated to theirs, in footsteps since
resurfaced and rerouted a bit, meaning I have to trespass
somehow. But for once, I managed to get everything to
align perfectly; the exact car, the exact track and the right
bits of paperwork allowing me to indulge myself. Ayrton
Senna da Silva announced his arrival at the highest level
of the European racing scene when he was invited to take
part in a race marking the opening of the then new
Nürburgring Grand Prix circuit, in a recently launched
Mercedes-Benz 190E 2.3 16V Cosworth. Quite some
footsteps to follow in.

Ben is a mate of mine from up North. Straight-talking,
hard-driving and self-deprecating, when he told me about
the cheap Mercedes-Benz 190E 2.3 16V Cosworth he'd
bought, I knew exactly what I wanted to do with it. He'd
also bought a MK2 Vauxhall Cavalier cabriolet and I knew
what I wanted to do to that too, and it involved fire. The
Mercedes was special though. They spent £600 million on
the development of the car and it was launched in 1982.
By their own admission, it was massively over-
engineered. But it wasn't a sports car. Mercedes were
getting thrashed in rallying by the new Audi Quattro and
enlisted British engineering business Cosworth to work
their magic. In 1983, they released the 190E 2.3-16,

informally known as the Mercedes 190E Cosworth. Many cars in this book are rented. Some are blagged. This car was scrounged.

Eighteen owners is quite a few. It's easy to imagine the first owner, carefully specifying extras (in the case of Ben's car, that included the smaller 'sport' steering wheel) and excitedly awaiting delivery, then lavishing care on their new car during their ownership. Then the subsequent owner picking up the car after some depreciation and perhaps saving money by having a local specialist work on it, then owners three, four and five, perhaps having a garage do the serious spannering but doing the basics themselves, moving it on when bigger bills loomed. The miles adding up, car getting tired. Owner six might have fixed it on his driveway. Owner seven didn't bother with preventative maintenance and used Chinese tyres bought off Gumtree. Owner eight bought a bargain, riddled with the little things the previous cheapskate never fixed, ignored warning lights, rattle can-painted over the rust and drove the car like Senna himself (I'm getting on to him soon) because they knew the thing was on it's last legs anyway. Then imagine ten more owners after that. Ten. Each one driving everywhere with the words "If you no longer go for a gap that exists, you are no longer a racing driver" in their head. That takes the total to 18 owners and Ben, who, thanks to the Merc's many seemingly incurable ailments, bought it for peanuts. It was christened Merscabies. He loaned it to me on the understanding that if it broke, I'd have to get it fixed. Quite a risky deal for me.

Senna should not have been there, but after fellow Brazilian Emerson Fittipaldi dropped out, he was invited to join a who's who in F1 lineup of drivers to celebrate the opening of the new Nürburgring with a one-make 12-lap race. Mercedes supplied 20 identical examples of their new 190E Cosworth as a hugely expensive way of launching their new model to the world. At that moment, Senna was 'only' British F3 champion and had had a few outings in a Toleman in F1. Niki Lauda was the focus of the media, having suffered his burns on the dangerous old circuit and being a vocal supporter of the new one, considered much safer. He was racing but missed qualifying and started last.

Mercedes were so confident that Lauda would win the race that they had an identical car, stickers and all, ready to be placed in their museum before the race took place. The lineup included James Hunt (probably still pissed up from the generous German hospitality the night before), Senna's later nemesis, Alain Prost, Denny Hulme, Reutemann, Brabham, Watson, de Angelis and Rosberg (Keke, not Nico). There were also German touring car champions, taking the total amount of entrants to 20. You'll find the actual race on YouTube somewhere.

Thanks to the selfish pigdogs who employed me at the time, I could not get away from England until late evening on the Friday, having negotiated (for a not inconsiderable fee) exclusive access to the Nürburgring Grand Prix circuit for a precious few minutes very early on Saturday. I fell into bed at 4 am, woke up at 6 am and went to the track to follow in Senna's footsteps exactly 20 years to the day after the Race of Champions originally took place.

The car was driving rather nicely. It has mechanical fuel injection and sounds rather rorty, a bit carb-like, and encouraged ragged driving. Ben had bought it cheap because probably a dozen or so of the previous owners had failed to cure a fuelling issue. He had it sorted and, sun-warped vinyl trim aside, it felt every bit as over-engineered as it's reputation claimed. It wasn't very fast though. Having been developed to rally, it was then employed in touring car action, where it invariably came second best to the BMW E30 M3. Still, this is the one I'd have. 185 bhp is pretty paltry by sporting saloon standards of today and 0–60 mph in about 8 seconds must have had Senna praying for some divine assistance.

Today, to drive, they feel like an old mechanical car, things click and clunk, you can almost feel the engine sucking air, feel the combustion through your fingers in the wheel and lean on the tyres through the corners. And it does lean a bit too. Watching the old footage of the race, the cars were pitching about. Alan Jones and James Hunt cut corners and drove across the grass. de Angelis came in with lumps hanging off his car. They all got stuck in and, as we all now know, Senna came in first.

The Nürburgring seems to be in an eternal state of financial turmoil. There's a spectacularly rubbish shopping mall where you can buy Ferrari-branded ashtrays, wonder at the white elephant roller coaster that has barely ever moved and go to a visitor centre about a racetrack that you may as well actually see and experience first hand yourself a few hundred metres away. The management were particularly tricky to deal with but, considering they were probably broke, let me hire the F1 part of the track for a couple of hundred quid but on the understanding that I first met with their management team. Germans love admin. I took, all the way from England, a birthday cake to celebrate the anniversary of the place opening. We met, they offered coffee and paperwork, and I slipped out the cake, stuck in and lit some candles, then sung "happy birthday, dear Nürburgring", in German. I thought it was a nice idea. The cake was a bit squashed and the candles set off a smoke alarm. No one even smiled, the miserable bastards.

I was allowed on the track for two hours. During that time, for safety purposes, I was to be shadowed by a safety car. It was a white Jaguar XJR on German plates, piloted by some young blonde-haired fellow who looked like he would be more at home in a Messerschmitt. Shooting errant Englishmen, like me. We had radios. On to the track, up to speed and with the sun shining, I imagined the roar of the crowd at the original Race of Champions. "Nein! Bitte sechzig", shouted my minder. 60 kph.

I pulled the trick all speeding Brits abroad used and did 60 mph (100 kph), pretending not to know the difference and waited for him to catch up. It didn't take long. "KPH, nicht MPH!" I pulled over. I explained that we'd driven a very long way in a very knackered car to pay homage to one of the greatest names in motorsport. We agreed I could go 100 mph. No more. This was actually asking a lot of the old Merscabies and it forced me to focus on my driving. No braking unless you're in the scenery, steering angles so acute in corners that the car leant over and clipped its tyre valves on the apex. Maybe. Well, it felt that way.

My two hours flew by. I did not time the laps; I just hung on, chucking the car around in an increasingly aggressive fashion. Senna had been here, in this car. It felt very special.

My time was up. Senna went on to win 41 Grands Prix and three drivers' championships. I went on to (or, rather, back to) utter obscurity in England, but had loved my time following in Senna's footsteps. The Merscabies was sold on and now lives with another friend, who rarely uses it, and it's looking for its twentieth owner. I'd rather see this one in the Mercedes museum than Senna's own car; it has achieved (and withstood) more than Senna ever did with his.

The island of New Skegness

It started in a bar with two friends. Let's call them Andre and Simon, for those are their names. The sun was shining, we had enjoyed a few drinks on the quayside and Andre was trying to stay on fizzy pop as he was showing off his new boat. Drink driving is a serious crime and, in this corner of Scandinavia, drink sailing is viewed just as harshly. The parallel with driving goes further. Much as owners of new sports cars look for a blast up the bypass to show off their new machinery, we cajoled Andre into taking us on an adventure somewhere on his boat. We three piled aboard and set sail into the Oslofjørd. Provisions included gin and some cans of a disgusting local lager called Aass. Those who find the name amusing may wish to know that there are variations of this brew called Aass Classic and Aass Lite. It all tastes like aass.

Boaties will tell you that, close to shore, there is a speed limit, but out on the open seas, you can play at being a Class 1 powerboat racer. This boat was powered by a whopping outboard, was about 20 feet long and had one of those canopies with a hundred press studs that make the roof on a Caterham look weatherproof. Banging through the waves at speed, we charged about aimlessly, slewing around doing great big aquatic skids, before slowing to look at some of the thousands of islands along the broken coastline. Sweden was somewhere over to our left, Norway to the right and ahead was Denmark. Some of this is nature reserve. Now and then, a huge ferry would waft by in the distance. We had no idea where we were. There was a depth radar on the bridge but it didn't seem as reliable as peering into the clear deep waters yourself. On the bottom were crabs and shells and beds of seaweed. Picking your way through the islands was difficult. Some were smooth, flat bits of rock that barely broached the surface, and there were many jagged rocks just beneath the surface. One of the islands had a tank painted on it. A full-sized tank. We went for a look. There were others nearby with strange markings and some odd wooden posts and things, but not a soul nor sign of life anywhere.

I love sailing but am rubbish at it. Pull a rope to go quicker, let it go to slow, pull another string to go left, release to go right, and have your skull stoved in by the boom and/or get drowned when you get any of this even a little bit wrong. There are no brakes. Duisberg is not a name to be added to a long list of notable British sailors; Admiral Nelson, Captain Cook and Sir Francis Drake, a man who died of dysentery in Panama. I wonder if he'd been drinking Aass. It was doing strange things to my shipmates already. Booze had them staggering about on land, yet their internal gyroscopes had somehow synchronised with the swell on the boat and they walked about perfectly stabilised.

Gin and sunshine combined in my head and, to give this pleasant but otherwise aimless sailing trip a purpose, I decided to do my bit for Queen and country. It had been probably a century since anywhere was added to the British Empire. Nauru became the last little bit of pink added to the map in 1919 after the Germans got kicked off and we needed the phosphate there. Growing up in England, we were taught the Empire exploited those in the Third World, damaged the Earth's natural resources and that, in general, colonialism is a bad thing. Like young Germans bored of being nagged about the Nazis, it's easy to get a bit miffed with being blamed for my ancestors' antics overseas. So I decided to invade what became to be known as New Skegness.

The photograph (alas, there is but one) makes it look bigger than it is. I guess it's 30 metres long by about 5 wide. Its highest peak might be 3 metres above sea level. I informed my shipmates of my intentions, to claim the virgin territory for Her Maj, and, armed with a Union Jack nailed to a broom handle, stood on the bow and guided the boat close to shore. Thanks to the action of the currents and water, there is a slow, drunken delay in a vessel responding to its controls. Thanks to the action of the Aass, there was a slow, drunken delay in Andre responding to my instructions. I fell off the boat and half onto the island, half in the bastard-cold water. I hoped for hula-hula girls showering me with flower garlands. There was a seagull with a gammy eye which flew off. I wedged the flag in a crevice and proclaimed myself Emperor.

I would struggle to find my island again, but am pretty sure it lay in Norwegian waters. Simon, shouting from the bow as they tried to back the boat closer to the island without snagging it on submerged rocks, reckoned that the reason the place was deserted and that there were tanks painted on things was because it was a military firing range. If we were shipwrecked here, would anyone ever find us? The population of New Skegness tripled as the lads eventually made it ashore, kicking my Union Jack over and talking in foreign. I feared for my island's sovereignty. I explained to them that this is now a British overseas protectorate and, if I had any phone signal, I would call up the Royal Air Force who would send over a squadron of Vulcans and bomb some sense into them. Here, on New Skegness, we are to speak English and respect our heritage. They skulked off up the other end of the island, drinking Aass and muttering things. A line was drawn. They got the northern end, I got the southern end. They held a poll, 100% turnout, all voting for independence from New Skegness. They wanted to do a deal with the North Koreans. I was more concerned that the boat was floating off. Mineral extraction rights were discussed, which I think meant ownership of the seagull cack. There was talk of hosting a Grand Prix and building a duty-free shop. Then, disaster struck—the gin ran out.

The seas around New Skegness abound with wildlife. A deep sea, with huge cod and beautiful mackerel, and crabs, langoustine and lobster scuttling about deep below. And the skies are full of geese flying effortlessly in the cold air over ducks bobbing in the waves. And they're all easily killed and taste delicious, said Simon, having worked up an appetite after his mutiny. The boat drifted back a bit closer. Andre had found a sharp stick and looked hungry. The wildlife looked in danger. The British overseas protectorate known as South New Skegness decided to hold an amnesty with it's driving-on-the-wrong-side-of-the-road northern neighbour, and got the boat back. A long and meandering journey back to port took quite some time. The population of New Skegness moored up in time for last orders. It couldn't take any more Aass. Brandy was called for plus whatever the chef could rustle up at this late hour for three cold, wet and hungry colonists. "New boat?", the barman asked. "Yes. And a new country". If anyone sailing the Oslofjørd spots a little island with a union jack stuck on it, could you kindly let me know where it is exactly. New Skegness might be missing its Emperor.

Back to the future

Car;   Borrowed DeLorean DMC-12. 88 mph
                looks unlikely from behind the wheel of
                one.

Location;   Houston, USA.

Duration;   One day plus a serious slog to get over
                there and back.

Back to the Future was released in 1985 and I owe this
film quite a lot. You know the plot, you know the car. I
bore a passing resemblance to its hero, Marty McFly, and
Sharon who sat next to me in English at school had always
fancied him. Teenage hormones were raging. I invested in
a bodywarmer and some white trainers (only Hi-Tec,
because I was poor). I wore them to school and spoke
with my best attempt at an American accent and acted in
the frantic manner of a young man trying to get back to
the future. I must have looked like a colossal prat, but she
loved it. I'll spare you the details but I recall the
disappointment on her face. The boy, Marty McDuisberg,
became a *man* because of that film.

This was a long time ago. Back then, the chances of me
getting to even sit in a DeLorean were zero. I was too
young to appreciate that it was really just an Esprit,
saddled with a weedy engine and decorated with stainless
steel panels, half-arsedly slung together by Northern
Irishmen with no experience of building cars. People love
them, even to this day, but I cannot understand how
they're apparently worth more than an equivalent Esprit.
Maybe it's the film appearance. That film did wonders for
everyone, it seems. Now, being old, it is much easier to be
taken seriously when trying to borrow keys to an

interesting car. The factory in Dunmurry closed down when the financial façade crumbled, Mr. DeLorean was involved in a drug sting operation, Lotus' Colin Chapman died of a heart attack, the accountant got sent down and, really, that would have been the end of it—but for the film.

Many characters in this book may seem like caricatures, talked up by an author keen to give colour to these flimsy pages, but they're all real and as described. Steve Wynn (hello, if you're reading this) is every bit as colourful as this description; his hair and teeth are suspiciously good, he looks tanned and healthy, and wears suits that look like they're from BHS c.1989 but are probably really expensive. He says he drives a DeLorean. He drives a Jaguar. He has an accent that starts out at the beginning of a conversation as Texan, which slowly fades before finishing as Scouse. Steve is an ex-pat who set up shop repairing old French and British stuff in Texas before finding that people came to him with DeLoreans when they knew he could fix the smoky old PRV engine. Peugeot, Renault and Volvo (hence the acronym) joined forces to build this V6 in 1974. Nearly a decade on, this old lump was pressed into service in DeLoreans and owners came to Steve when they shat themselves—the engines, not the owners. Spotting an opportunity, as spotty teens who loved the film started earning money in IT and actually had money to buy the car, Steve bought the remains of the company and started building them from old but unused parts. I went to see him. I had to try one. Not because of the film, but for what the film had done for me.

In a suburb of Houston sits the DeLorean factory. Outside is a huge row of cars. It looks like a car factory but would be more accurately described as a car servicing workshop. The cars are either for sale or in for some work. In the reception is a pinball machine inspired by the film, a chassis and drivetrain (it is distinctive Lotus double Y-shaped layout), original pictures and posters from the company, some rare parts on display and other interesting bits and bobs. They buy and strip old cars and there's a fantastic relic; a door from the last car made in Dunmurry with, inside the cavity behind the trim, a hand-written message from the men who built it, lamenting the last ever car to be made by them.

Steve talks excitedly about making an EV version, a GRP-bodied version with a better engine (that'll be an Esprit then) and other ideas. His hair doesn't move and there's barely a wrinkle on him anywhere. Even at the time of writing (early 2017), there are words on Wikipedia about restarting volume production. Steve is a salesman. He gave me the keys to a car for a drive. Why had I gone to such trouble, travelling so far, to drive a car I know is fundamentally flawed? Well, it's like going on a date with the pinup of your oversexed and underachieving teenage years. After years of lusting after someone famous, finally finding out they're single and available, *and* up for a fumble. I wanted to try the car. I didn't dress up like McFly and there were enough silly accents already. "Cheers", and I was off.

I saw her in an off-licence a year or two ago. I noticed her because of the pack of feral kids at her heels and the way she struggled with lots of really full carrier bags about to split in each hand, yet was trying to get a pack of Stella Artois under her arm and simultaneously claim for a winning scratchcard. Time had not been kind. I passed with a smile, nothing more needed, she had her hands full. That was Sharon. I would not want to revisit my first time with her any more than I'd like to own a DeLorean today. Yes, they're distinctive and memorable, but so is Sharon's tattoo of the Nottingham Forest crest on her neck. I'm sure she'd be as disparaging about me (then and now).

They made 8500-ish examples of the DMC-12 and most still survive. One went back to Lotus for some evaluation but they destroyed it. On occasionally meeting Lotus employees today, they seem to prefer not to talk about DeLorean, perhaps embarrassed by this chapter in their history after Mr. Chapman diddled the British government out of millions on a project designed to put people into work in the troubles of Northern Ireland. There are a few right-hand-drive examples but nearly all are left-hookers, like the one I was driving. You probably love the car, I certainly love a flawed hero (like Chapman), but I can't love this.

The car, as I drove the concrete highway out of Houston, was rubbish. 88 mph and all that nonsense? Forget it. Sloshy automatic gear changes, no power, a whiff of smoke from the exhaust and a dull drone from behind my head somewhere. Even new, this model did 0–60 mph in over 10 seconds. Those gull-wing doors are just daft and the interior is overly 70s, and that's not good. All the wonderful driving characteristics of the Esprit seemed missing. It smelt funny and is not nice to be in. The car, not Sharon. She loved the film and would love the DeLorean. I'm happy to have met them in the past, but wouldn't want either of them in my future.

Chasing the ambulance chasers: part 2

Another spell in the office, unattended, mind wandering, radio stuck on some bloody awful local station with inane adverts for claims companies… I couldn't help myself. Here's the transcript of a chat 'Stephen Milligan' had.

Stephen Milligan: Hello. Could you help me ? I am looking for advice on making a personal injury claim for a recent accident.

Kenny: Hello Stephen, my name is Kenny and i am a Legal Consultant at YouClaim.

Stephen Milligan: My word, that was prompt!

Kenny: We try! What sort of information are you seeking?

Stephen Milligan: I am looking for advice on making a claim for compensation for a recent accident I had. Are you that kind of company ?

Kenny: Yes, what type of accident have you been involved in?

Stephen Milligan: It was a road traffic accident, that is to say, it was an accident, in the traffic, on a road.

Kenny: What are the circumstances surrounding the accident?

Stephen Milligan: It is all rather unpleasant, speaking frankly, if you are comfortable I will try to explain as best I can?

Kenny: Thats fine, alternatively if you would like you can provide me with a telephone number and i shall contact you to discuss the matter if you like?

Stephen Milligan: I shall explain : I was driving home from exercising my Alsatian, Fritz, on the common. I was returning via the High Street, driving at precisely 30mph, in good visibility, when I was involved in this Road Traffic Accident. I was left with severe bruising and an unpleasant cut, about 4" long, roughly in the shape of the Isle of Wight. What further info is required by yourself ?

Kenny: How did the actual RTA occur?

Stephen Milligan: As I mentioned, I was driving along, Fritz on the passenger seat, securely fastened, when I decided to tune into the wireless. Traffic was heavy, and... Sorry, before I continue, are you familiar with the road layout of the A3, near the roundabout, just past the Asda shopping place,or shall I just continue ?

Kenny: I'm not familiar with the layout of the A3, but please continue.

Stephen Milligan: Certainly Kenny. The A3, known as the Portsmouth Road for much of its length, is a dual carriageway, or expressway, which follows the historic route between London and Portsmouth passing close to Kingston upon Thames, Guildford, Haslemere and Petersfield. For much of its 67-mile (108 km) length, it is classified as a trunk road and, apart from a section within the London conurbation and short section where the Hindhead Tunnel is currently being built, is largely dual carriageway. At its southerly end, the original road has been replaced by the A3(M), but the designation A3 is still used to identify the old road. There's an Asda store on it, and a traffic island, this is the general vicinity of my deeply unpleasant accident. What further detail of my accident is required?

Kenny: Thanks for that information, very informative, how did the unpleasant accident occur?

Stephen Milligan: There was coming together of vehicles, on the road, near the Asda, in a position directly oblique to the island, parallel to where those blasted Travellers set up camp last year and left all manner of detritus, including dozens of refuse sacks and a poor pony with 3 legs tethered to the fence. I say pony, it may have been a mule, it was some time ago. In any case, I was driving my car (a pristine Austin Metro City in old English white), when I had this coming together with another car. I had no idea it would happen and have been in considerable discomfort ever since.

Kenny: How did this coming together occur? Did you collide with the other vehicle firstly? Or did he collide with you?

Stephen Milligan: Sorry for the delay there Kenny, meals on wheels tried to deliver, but I'm not eating Shepherds Pie so I told them to take it back. I was brutally rammed at the front by the other car who was stationary, the front bumper of 'Flynn' (my Austin Metro) suffered structural damage, and consequently the rear of the offender's car was heavily damaged. That is to say, we collided, with him being to blame of course. I can provide a sketch of this if required, or further detail on how he was distracted etc.

Kenny: So you collided with the rear of his vehicle? If this is the case we would be unable to assist you.

Stephen Milligan: No, quite the opposite in fact.

Kenny: So did he collide with the rear of your Austin Metro?

Stephen Milligan: No, I am sorry, perhaps I've confused you, please allow me to clarify. 'Flynn' (my Austin Metro) was rammed at the front, the resultant damage being a 3" (c.75mm) deep concave indentation and dislodging the front number plate. I was thrown forwards, face first, causing facial injuries that have left me looking rather like an elderly Boxer, similar to Cassius Clay (although I'm not of brown-skin myself you understand although I've nothing against them). The rear of the offenders car (a VolksWagen, I recall it was a fetching shade of blue, do you need the registration, I have it here somewhere) was heavily damaged as a result of colliding with the front of my car. They had been distracted and this, above all else, is the root cause of the accident.

Kenny: So were you stationary? Has the other party reversed into you vehicle? Did anybody witness this?

Stephen Milligan: Oh there were witnesses all right, there was a tall gentleman walking a whippet with a grey overcoat who walked with a limp, he saw everything. He gave me his name, it is Tony Smith. There was a orbidly obese woman in a tracksuit (oh, the irony), chain smoking, and a family of foreign looking types, shifty eyes, you know the type, probably from Poland. They didn't speak a word of English but I am quite sure they know how to claim benefits. I, on the other hand, have never claimed for anythingin my life, other than compensation for this wretched accident, and 10 years of incapacity benefit when I had virulent scabies.

Kenny: going back to the accident, were you stationary in your vehicle? Has the other party reversed into you? If this is not the case i cant see how the accident has occurred.

Stephen Milligan: Immediately after the accident we were both stationary, prior to that there was considerable movement, perhaps upwards and in excess of 10mph, perhaps 30 mph. Both forwards and backwards and c.15 degrees of lateral movement. It is rather difficult to tell as I was trying to avoid the silly VolksWagen driver at the time and neglected to accurately record my driving speed, although the accuracy of 'Flynn's speedometer may be in question as although I rarely travel at more than 30 MPH anywhere due to the horrendous cost of fuel, it has been some time since I had it's dials calibrated.

Kenny: So you have collided with the back of the Volkswagen? If this is the case it appears you would be at fault for the accident.

Stephen Milligan: No. The back of the VolksWagen collided with me. I fail to see how you draw your conclusion from the facts stated. Here is a diagram, with X representing my car, and Y representing the VW. The - symbol representes the road and the O symbol is the roundabout and # being the watching family of illegal immigrants. -------------X------Y-0-#---------------- then in the aftermath we arrived at --------------Y-X-------0-----#------ with the # a bit further away as they were going to the DFS store as they had some kind of '0% finance' offer on, or something, where there wild-eyed children could get a free balloon and some cordial to drink for free. I hope this is clear. Regarding my compensation, can you send cash, instead of a cheque, as my bank are currently being rather obstructive over an administrative matter, blasted Indian call centre and whatnot.

Stephen Milligan: Hello ?

Chat session has been terminated by the site operator.

Remembering Albert Ball

Car;   Scrounged Morgan 3 Wheeler. The closest thing to flying without leaving the ground.

Location;   Home to Saint-Omer, France.

Duration;   A weekend.

Nottingham Castle is funny. American tourists, fresh from a trip to Sherwood Forest, often pop in to 'Notting-haam' to see what they probably expect to be a fairytale castle with moats and turrets and largely leave disappointed when learning that the old castle was pulled down years ago to make way for a stately home. It's a nice spot regardless, and in the grounds is a statue of a local hero; Captain Albert Ball, VC, DSO & Two Bars, MC.

On the Morgan Motor Company website, there's a scratchy black and white picture of Albert Ball, sat in his newly purchased 3 Wheeler, taken in 1917. It's a slightly awkward-looking, staged photograph. He sits in uniform, looking sideways at the camera, an unwilling hero. His car is a little different to the modern 3 Wheeler but built in the same factory in Great Malvern, Worcestershire, and the design ethos is much the same. The construction techniques probably haven't moved on that much either. Getting your hands on press car keys isn't easy when you're an ordinary chap like me, but when I told Morgan I wanted to pay tribute to Albert Ball in my own special way, they needed little convincing.

The lady at Nottingham City Council kindly arranged to open the gates to let my car in, to park under the statue of Albert Ball. It was early November, cold and wet. This is the kind of car you can drive through ornamental gardens, down pathways and under trees, with tourists smiling and taking photos in the teeming rain. Ball's statue shows him as the hero, looking to the horizon, with biplanes carved into the base. He never wanted to be a hero. He lived on nearby Lenton Boulevard and had a happy childhood of climbing trees, riding a motorbike and shooting an air rifle. As war broke out, he, like so many others buoyed by patriotism, joined the Sherwood Foresters. He soon transferred to the Royal Flying Corp.

As you can see from the pictures, there is no roof on a Morgan 3 Wheeler. It has a tiddly aero screen and no heater. It has too much power and not enough grip. The turning circle is huge and I have a theory that the front tyres are sourced from a motorbike and don't have enough lateral strength for hard cornering. The air-cooled S&S V-Twins of early examples explode because they were designed to be installed in one orientation in a 'bike, with the leading cylinder facing forwards and is naturally cooled more than the one behind it, so the ECU is programmed to fuel the twin cylinders differently. In the Morgan, mounted sideways, the cylinders get an equal amount of cold air but the ECU was not reprogrammed, so they're not quite fuelled the same, eventually leading to one getting hotter than the other, and things potentially going bang.

The roll hoop behind your head is sturdy, but unless you're a midget, it only comes to the nape of your neck if you roll it over. Rolling it over isn't difficult to do. The chassis is set up for understeer, probably in the name of safety. So enthusiastic idiots like me, who like to hang a tail out, are obliged to give it a Scandinavian flick to get it going, which results in odd behaviour from those peculiar front tyres and, surprisingly easily in my experience, the whole thing quickly digs in and lifts a front wheel. And I don't mean an inch or so; I mean the whole car tips at some mad angle with a front wheel a foot off the deck. The passenger will have an angular lump of steel sticking in their knee, the standard steering wheel is too big and you'll forget to cancel the indicators and drive around confusing other road users. Look at the length of this paragraph, all knocking the car, and I've not even finished. The filler cap key slot is tight and feels like the key will bend in the lock. The petrol gauge expresses the tank's contents as an opinion, as opposed to a fact, and in percentages on a digital gauge hidden in a menu. It does say 'WARNING HOT' on the engine and exhaust but, to an idiot like me, such words mean 'TOUCH THIS', with scorching results. It has too much power in too narrow a power band so it drives digitally—power is on or off. It is far too fast and is easily blown about by passing lorries. The noise of that engine will either delight your neighbours or have them try and get you ASBO'd. The brakes are almost good enough. That natty starter switch, inspired by the trigger on a military aircraft, will swivel about in the dash. When parking overnight, there's a tonneau cover held in place with press studs that will rip your nails off. When you return to the car in the morning, the tonneau will be gone and some apologetic randomer will be sat in the car making 'brum' noises. To get in, shoo them out then cock a leg over the side, stand on the seat, slide down and regret that you didn't dry your feet first as you invariably have a wet arse. People will mob you every time you stop and ask inane questions. And yet, I consider every fault nothing but a quirk, every failure a foible and every design shortcoming simply a charming facet of Morgan ownership. When it tries to kill me, I consider it is just showing it's true character and forgive it, like a man besotted with a beautiful but crazy lover. I am utterly besotted with the Morgan 3 Wheeler and any time with one is precious.

It pissed it down in Nottingham. The kind of rain that leaves you sodden in seconds, every fibre of your clothing heavy with cold, clammy moisture, through to your underwear. The man from BBC Radio Nottingham couldn't get his microphone to work because of the noise of the rain. The woman from the telly wouldn't even get out of the fogged-up crew van. Those who had turned up to see me off on a trip to France, for Remembrance Day, were beaten by the weather. Utterly drenched in the footwell was a poppy wreath. My destination was over 300 miles away, in another country. As I left the stop–start traffic of Nottingham, I used a sponge to soak up the puddles inside, emptying it over the side as I drove, like a fisherman bailing out a leaky boat.

Winding the car up to motorway speeds and hunkering down in the seat, I could tilt my head to one side of the aeroscreen and put my face in a small pocket where the air scooped the rain out of the way. In such weather, logically, one should drive slowly and passively, allowing for greater stopping distances and giving other road users space to make mistakes. It's not easy to spot a little machine like this and lorries, in particular, rarely seem to see you until you're past. But in such weather conditions, I just wanted to go quicker. To beat the conditions. Every mph more I could manage meant reaching warmth and safety that little bit sooner. Albert Ball, in his aircraft, suffered rotten conditions far worse than this. I drove, totally flat out, to Dover and Eurotunnelled to Calais.

Albert Ball was an unwilling hero. He wasn't like other
pilots. He often slept in a tent on the airfield to be near
his aircraft, was a Christian and quickly came to resent his
success in shooting down Axis enemies. He wrote to his
father to say he was beginning to feel like a murderer.
And yet, with 1 million men dead or injured in the Battle
of the Somme, the British government needed a hero.
And they focussed on the men whose results were
seemingly so easily measured and published. The men in
the air. Pilots like Albert Ball. But he hated the attention.
He was a loner. He was credited with 44 victories but
wrote, "I hate this game, but it is the only thing one must

do just now". The Morgan must have been a happy distraction, a reward for living such a wretched existence. I hate to see the word 'glory' used in memorials. "To the glorious dead". There is no glory in a death like this and I struggle to comprehend the reasons why millions of men gave their lives in this conflict. I was not making my trip in the name of patriotism—Ball was an unwilling hero anyway. I wanted to show my respect to a local man who, like me, loved his Morgan.

Even in such ugly conditions, I loved driving this car. A car like this impresses at car meets, but I hate car meets. You stand in a pub car park with strangers, not being able to drink because you're driving, even though you're not driving anywhere as you're stood listening to men in jeans and trainers talking about paint codes and trim specifications of cars that were designed to be enjoyed, while they occasionally rev an engine and irritate the regulars inside the pub. Cars are designed to be *driven*, for God's sake, but road trips need a reason and I like to think Albert Ball would have approved of mine, duct-taped GB sticker and all.

There's a grave in the military cemetery where he was laid to rest in the village of Annœullin, but the story of Ball's end lies in an obscure muddy field a mile or so away. Parking the Morgan on a small road, I traipsed across a wet field of rotting roots and crops that missed the harvest. In the middle of the field, scarcely visible from the road, is an engraved stone. This marks the spot where Ball crashed after a final dogfight, with Lothar von Richthofen, brother of the Red Baron. Ball emerged from a low cloud, inverted and died on impact. Not shot down but probably disorientated from endless combat, perhaps unaware that he had outlived the average of 18 hours his peers managed before succumbing. He was just 20 years old. Ball's father, on hearing the news, bought this field from the farmer and erected the stone, gifting the field back to the French on the understanding that the stone must never be moved. There, I laid a wreath.

There is an incredible joy in driving a car like this, on public roads, at speed. As one big, happy Europe, our lives are regulated, monitored and improved, whether we like it or not. It's inconceivable that we would ever face such a war again and, yet, the rough edges of life, the colour and the danger are now often taken away from us. This car has almost identical weight, power and speed as the WW1 aircraft piloted by the likes of Ball. It is hand-made by men with funny accents who hammer, plane and chisel away to make something magical.

There will come a day, probably in my lifetime, when cars like this will no longer be allowed to be made. I don't wish to sound UKIP-y, but legislation and well-meaning leaders will, some day, stop us from hurtling about in machines with no safety equipment and no tangible reason for existence other than to entertain the man or woman behind the wheel. The Morgan is a firm two fingers up to this. As our castles crumble and memories of heroes fade, it's crucial to champion such machines, to find a reason to use them so they live on that little bit longer. As Ball himself famously said, "It's the closest thing to flying without leaving the ground".

A distinguished gentleman on the telly

Car;   Loaned Morgan 3 Wheeler. More fun
                than you can imagine.

Location;   London, England.

Duration;   One day's driving, one night's drinking.

I wanted to be on the telly. Like many other chapters in
this book and, indeed, my entire life, this little adventure
started with booze and piss-taking. I'll start with the
latter. Many years ago, as an April Fools' Day joke, I
created a spoof company newsletter for the Morgan
Motor Company. It wasn't intended to be malicious, but I
could see why Charles Morgan sent me a slightly bitter
message about it soon afterwards. 'Mog Musings' was a
play on those dull one-page company newsletters little
businesses self-publish. Mine, for Morgan, had notices
about banning pipesmoke in the canteen ("that means
you, Margaret") and offers of a lift share from someone
commuting by bicycle. I don't remember much else. It
wasn't *that* funny but it (and, therefore, I) caught the
attention of Mr. Morgan himself and he was a bit miffed. I
have since met him and he's a lovely chap. Anyway, on to
the booze.

Me, my young daughter and the head of a foreign TV
channel (who must remain nameless in case this chapter
inspires other to copy me) were having drinks in a pub
overlooking the Thames. I had stalked this guy for some
time. He commissioned TV programmes about
motorbikes but had no money and I had ideas for telly
that no one else would touch. I don't speak his particular
flavour of foreign, so my daughter was taken out of
school for a 'dental appointment'. I had asked for a short

meeting, in the pub, to run my idea past Señor X. In order to overcome any cultural or linguistic difficulties, I got him sloshed. So, me, a drunk foreigner and a skiving schoolgirl who was two years off her GCSEs sat together and all agreed a deal whereby he would show one of my films on the basis that he didn't have to pay me. We shook hands, he nearly fell over some railings into the river and we all went home happy.

Back to Morgan. Following my little faux pas, I assumed I would be blacklisted by them, but having written a few nice things about them lately for a few magazines (I was well into the swing of writing for car mags now), they had forgiven me. I had the feeling they wanted to put their magnificent 3 Wheeler in front of the biker audience somehow, on the telly. They could have commissioned an advert but they're bloody expensive to make and, honestly, who watches adverts anyway? I convinced them that I would make a film for them, an advertorial. All they needed to do was cover the costs and give me a car. They agreed. Sober, too.

The Distinguished Gentleman's Ride is a charity motorbike shindig, held in various cities around the world simultaneously, in aid of men's health charities. It is huge. In London alone, there were almost 1000 bikers. And me. I have not ridden a motorbike since I fell off Carl Biddle's Honda Cub in the 1980s round the back of the Air Cadets' hut. I have no motorbike licence and no motorbike. The Morgan 3 Wheeler is so universally loved that it was permitted entry, as was I, and I had paid a film-making mate (Nick) to turn up with a camera. This was going to be the film that got me on telly. Nick couldn't film and drive at the same time, so, him being an athletic sort, we had a plan. He would run between tube stations, popping up as we passed, and jump on the next tube to stay ahead of us. I booked stuff and went to London.

At this point, being given free use of one of my all-time favourite cars, having my own little slot on some foreign TV channel, getting paid by a company I once publicly took the piss out of, filming on-the-fly with no kit and not even being able to afford transport for my cameraman, I really should have been satisfied. Fortunately, the school didn't believe the playground rumours about my daughter's day off hammering out TV deals in a London pub with exotic foreign businessmen and accepted the fib about the dentist. I should have played it safe, spent the previous evening studying my script and the route, and had an early night. But I was on a roll. And I was on expenses.

I booked a rather nice hotel, invited my dangerous blonde girlfriend and, remembering this was all on expenses, got drunk. Mind-bendingly, oh-my-word-I-am-never-drinking-again drunk, to celebrate my good fortune. We woke up 30 minutes *after* the essential safety briefing had started, miles away, with a million missed calls from the frantic cameraman wondering what he was to film without us and our car. I was a bit sick in the sink. I tied my cravat and encouraged the blonde to put her slap on pronto before we jumped in the Moggy and made it to the safety briefing an hour after it finished, looking like a dishevelled pair of alcoholic aristocrats. This gig was not only about the bikes but about style too. There was to be no racing, no willy-waving, no drag-strip silliness. The intention was to gather a large group of retro bike riding and well-dressed ladies and distinguished gentleman. Fortunately, I looked like a gentleman, even if I hadn't behaved like one.

From the start in Lea Valley, the bikes charged off south towards the Thames, along the Embankment, past Big Ben and the Houses of Parliament, and up to Regent's Park. The Mog may be quick enough, but bikes do that lane-splitting thing and the blonde and I spent more time snogging in traffic than getting anywhere.

The convoy of bikes was brilliant. From mopeds to scramblers, bobbers, motorbike and sidecar combos, all of a certain vintage and piloted by people who had travelled from all over England to join us. You sit low in a 3 Wheeler and the bike engines at ear level were deafening. It was a hoot. Cameraman Nick popped up here and there and got the footage needed, tourists took selfies with us, crowds smiled and the day was capped by the most beautiful little drift around Parliament Square while the bobbies smiled and turned a blind eye. Well, it *is* for charity, after all, officer.

The car was returned, the blonde went home and I pondered giving CPR to Nick who had effectively ran a half-marathon while simultaneously trying to film hundreds of things. But I had arrived late and, as a result of that, and not being able to afford a camera car, we didn't have enough footage. Even with some slow-mos added, gratuitous lingering shots of London's spectacular architecture and, of course, lots of shots of people with half-foot-long 'taches, the finished film was too short. Would *Televisiones Productiones Globales* (not their real name) show it at all? Would Morgan think I'd played another practical joke on them and there was no TV exposure? I was quite worried. I had also set off a few cameras enjoying myself and the car was making an unfamiliar suspension-related *thrub-thrub-thrub* noise from the rear somewhere when it went back. I panicked. Then went to the pub.

We need a 30-minute film in order to show it once, said Mr. TV via email, via my young translator. I had 4 minutes. I panicked some more. He watched it anyway. He loved it. Its short length was, in the end, a blessing in disguise. It got used as a filler between other programmes, shown not once, but 90 times. Each time it was shown, it had at least 50000 viewers. 4.5 million times our film was watched in the first month after release alone and it still crops up on telly now and then. I was off the hook. Morgan were delighted. I felt like I had repaid them in full after my earlier piss-taking and had had a blast. To date, this episode represents perhaps my greatest blag yet. *And* I got my ugly chops on the telly.

Caught by the fuzz?

This is <u>not</u> a chapter on law avoidance. On trips like these, there's a reasonable chance that the local police might take an interest in your antics. They know where to lurk. They're drivers too, remember. With the right destination, there is usually plenty of space to stretch your car without getting into a spot of bother. Remember, abroad, the police can take your licence, which is a big deal for foreign types but means little to Brits as the DVLA will post you a new one if you tell them you lost it. You'll need another driver with a licence (and insurance) to move a car if they take your licence, so hop in someone else's car and tell the rental company where to find yours. There is no reciprocal agreement regarding points between Brits and the rest of the EU (all details correct at time of going to print, pre-Brexit), although fines are payable locally and speed camera shenanigans are irrefutably linked to the credit card you gave the rental company. Don't muck about, if you get a fine—pay it. But it's best to avoid picking one up in the first place.

I have, in my time, collected tickets in the UK (Congestion Charge in a Rover Metro and the Dartford Crossing in a Porsche), France (speeding in a Peugeot something), Belgium (speeding in a VW Golf) and Germany (speeding in a Ford Galaxy and a verbal warning for accidentally racially abusing a police officer when I panicked and my German came out all wrong). I am not condoning any of this. I have friends in the force in both Blighty and the colonies and know the rules. Still, if you get stuck and you don't speak the local lingo, here's a set of phrases which might just come in handy. The English first, then the foreign thereafter.

Italian

Good morning/afternoon, Officer.

Buongiorno/pomeriggio, Ufficiale.

I am English/Scottish/Welsh/Irish/Rhodesian, and I am on a driving holiday.

Sono inglese/scozzese/gallese/Irlanda/Rhodesian, e io sono su una vacanza in auto.

No, it is not mine, do I look like I'd buy a diesel Corsa?

No, non è mio, posso apparire come avrei comprato un diesel Corsa?

The brake lights DO work.

Le luci dei freni funzionano.

I saw that! You just smashed it!

L'ho visto! Basta fracassato esso!

I bloody saw you.

Ti ho visto, bastardo.

I can't breathe, I can't breathe!

Non riesco a respirare, non riesco a respirare!

Not the face, please not the face!

Non la faccia, non la faccia!

It's a Rolex. Take it!

Si tratta di un Rolex. Prendilo!

German

Hello Officer.

Hallo Offizier.

Yes, here is my licence and rental agreement.

Ja, hier ist meine Lizenz und Mietvertrag.

About 60.

Etwa 60.

mph. Which is about 40 kph, right?

mph. Üngefahr 40 kph, nicht wahr?

Yes, I did attend school.

Ja, ich habe die Schule besuchen.

It's not my fault if the German word for residential home for the elderly is almost the same as Nürburgring!

Es ist nicht meine Schuld, wenn das deutsche Wort für Wohnhaus für ältere Menschen fast die gleiche wie Nürburgring ist!

I did think it strange to see a mobility scooter on a racetrack.

Ich glaube es seltsam, eine Mobilitäts Roller auf einer Rennstrecke zu sehen.

Please pass my sincere condolences to the family.

Bitte leiten Sie meine aufrichtige Beileid an die Familie.

No, the handcuffs are not too tight.

Nein, die Handschellen sind nicht zu eng.

French

Hello, officer, how can I help you?

Bonjour, officier, comment puis-je vous aider?

Routine, you say? No problem.

Routine, dites-vous? Pas de problème.

It's open. Inside you will see a first aid kit, spare tyre, map, warning triangle and high-vis jackets for me and her, in accordance with French law.

C'est ouvert. A l'intérieur, vous verrez une trousse de premiers soins, roue de secours, carte, avertissement triangle et vestes haute à savoir pour moi et elle, en conformité avec la loi française.

My girlfriend.

Ma petite amie.

A size 8.

Une taille 8.

36 double D. I am concerned about your line of questioning.

36 doubles D. Je suis préoccupé par votre ligne de questionnement.

It doesn't look like frisking for drugs to me.

Il ne ressemble pas à gambader pour les médicaments pour moi.

And if I *don't* want to wait in your van?

Et si je ne veux pas attendre dans votre van?

Is that loaded?

Est-ce que chargé?

Yes, yes, I will wait!

Oui, oui, je vais attendre!

Some small print here. It should be pointed out that the author is: (a) not very good at foreign languages and (b) an idiot.

The thousand-pound Maserati

Car;   A 1986 Maserati Biturbo 425.

Location;   The Isle of Man.

Duration;   24 hours there plus half a day's travel
                either side.

No one reads the small print, but if you bother with it in this book, you'll see some arse-covering words about people's identities. Not here. Chris Rudge of Rotherham actually *is* Chris Rudge of Rotherham. I could describe him as a tall, dark and handsome ex-public schoolboy, but only if I wanted to hide his identity. Rudge is a mate of mine and, in an attempt to flog me his Maserati, we took it on a road trip to the Isle of Man. The reason more people don't visit the Isle of Man is the weather. It is a short and inexpensive ferry trip from mainland UK. There are lots of pubs. The roads, outside of inhabited areas, have no speed limits. It has a long and colourful history of racing. Why do people, at great expense, slog all the way to sit in the Nürburgring car park after yet another prang has probably closed it anyway, when such a brilliant place to drive is so near? Weather. It will piss down almost constantly if you visit. The Isle of Man has rainfall on 197 days a year compared to, say, London with 164 rainy days. London gets 594 millimetres of rain a year but the Isle of Man gets 1.1 metres of it. *Metres*!

As long as I can remember, Rudge has owned brilliantly rubbish cars. I should clarify what I mean by that. I mean cars that anyone with the tiniest amount of common sense wouldn't own but that stir the hearts of men like us. Ones that rot. Ones that won't start, or catch fire, or fall apart in new and fiendishly complex ways requiring obscenely expensive parts to repair. Cars like the Rover SD1, BMW 850, Alfa Romeo 155 and Maserati Biturbo. I love them all, totally, but am glad they decorate Rudge's front lawn instead of mine. Rudge knows I'm a sucker for anything with that fork on the grille and we booked a trip to the Isle of Man to give it a workout. The car was mine for £1000, if I wanted it. I really, really wanted it, but (unlike Rudge, who is quite handy with spanners) have no idea how to fix things.

The Maserati Biturbo is known by many names. The nomenclature is almost as complicated as the Super Mario plumbing of the induction system. The Biturbo was sold as a two-door coupe, a four-door saloon and as a convertible. The name is usually followed by a three-digit number. The first digit (a 2 or a 4) indicates the amount of doors and, therefore, body shape, and the second and third digits relate to the engine size (they were all V6s), apart from when there's a 'v' after the third digit, when it indicates how many valves the engine had, apart from the xx4v model, which had 24 valves, not 4. There were 2, 2.5 and 2.8 litre versions of the same V6. The convertible was built by Zagato and called Spyder, or Spider, or convertible. Most models from '81 to '86 were carb-fed, some were badged E for export or S or ES for no logical reason. Look at a photograph of what's under the bonnet. Look at all those hoses. And wires. Christ only knows what half of it does, and Christ is probably the only person with the divine powers needed to fix it when it borks.

The Isle of Man was a popular tourist resort in Victorian times but now seems to exist as a tax haven (Clarkson has a place here) and Mecca for mad bikers who come for the same reasons we did; to enjoy the open road. We ferried over with the Maserati. Only three of the four doors opened. I got in. It bounced, noticeably. Older cars like this always seem more softly sprung than modern stuff, don't they? I was making excuses for it already. The dead rear door couldn't be a big job to fix, or I could bodge the other rear door shut and call it a coupe. The rain was banging down on the car's roof and the inside smelled like a Scout hut. Damp was getting in somewhere and had been for some time. The roof lining is made, I think, from suede. In here, the cream colour was greyed in places by mould. I could probably rip that out and clean it, or maybe just dye it all grey to hide the rampant fungus. Rudge makes no excuse to hide any of this. We leave Douglas and join the circuit. There has been racing here since 1911. During the TT 'bike races between 1907 and 2015, there have been 246 fatalities on this very road.

The Maserati pitched and wallowed as we went. Coupled with the fungal fug, it was quite nauseating. The turbo power comes in hard and suddenly, nose lifting and the mismatched Chinese tyres all offer differing amounts of grip and worse feedback than a Ryanair customer satisfaction survey.

Most of the dials worked, but here, you need to be looking out, not glancing down, for the worker really did not give a stuff when he sullenly pushed these components together on a production line at the other end of Europe, at a time when ownership turbulence and shop-floor militancy meant that Luigi wasn't thinking how this car would perform nearly three decades later in a place like this.

The key to going quickly, safely, is looking ahead, not admiring the trident that seems to adorn everything in the cabin. Rudge, a Yorkshireman, has a brilliant turn of phrase. The seats were incredibly comfortable; "like sittin' on a fat bird's lap", he said. The gearbox was working but incredibly baggy. The gear knob would have shown that it was of a dog-leg configuration, but the markings on the wooden end were worn out. As I stirred the 'box looking for a gear, I asked Rudge, "dog-leg?" I had no idea where first was. "Snake-leg", he replied, knowing how vague the cogs were. We lurched up the mountainside at a very silly speed indeed, necks snapping with each change as all those leaky pipes gave boost seemingly when they felt like it.

Up the mountain, where everything is grey and glistening
wet, the kerbs are marked black and white to help you
spot turns and there are frequent roadside memorials to
the mad buggers who race here on two wheels every
year. The lap record for motorbikes is 16 minutes 53
seconds, an average of 133 mph over 37 miles by Michael
Dunlop. The lap record for cars is 17 minutes 49 seconds,
held by Mark Higgins driving an Impreza WRX STI, the
Subaru named after the acronym for sexually transmitted
infection, which is what I came down with after a day on
the Biturbo's suspiciously damp driver's seat. The road
winds between stone walls, chunky old cottages built up
against the road and trees that defy the weather, which
blows in sideways off the Irish Sea. Knowledge is key, of
course, and although I had been here before (in a Mini), I
was still not surprised to be doing 70 mph and being
overtaken by a delivery van which appeared from the
gloom behind and vanished into the gloom ahead in a
flash. "'ave 'im!", said Rudge. But I couldn't go quicker

here. We stopped at Peel for a pint, accidentally blocking someone in. "Can someone move that Cortina please?" The Biturbo isn't blessed with particularly good looks, is it? Neither is Rudge. We had a blast here and I regret not buying the car to this day, warts and all. I wonder if he still has that Lotus Excel?

As a postscript to this, Rudge has recently bought a Ford Cortina estate and a left-hand-drive Maserati Quattroporte with iffy paperwork.

The good, the bad and the oily: a BBC screen test

Car;   Only a model of a Metro this time.

Location;   London Motor Museum, England.

Duration;   One day, many takes.

No, not Top Gear. Around the time this all happened, Clarkson was punching people in the chops and getting fired, and the old TG show was falling to bits. Thousands of blokes were recording their audition tapes and sending them in, but I wasn't one of them. I'm simply not slick enough for that sort of show and I knew they'd have proper presenters lined up and, so it proved, the new team being decided fairly quickly. The only surprise being how natural Eddie Jordan's wig looked on camera and how much the public hated Chris Evans. I really like Chris Evans.

The Beeb knows that TG is a money-spinner and were looking at commissioning a further show. I was contacted by someone in the know who put me in touch with a production company that was putting together a pitch to BBC America for what they described as "a cross between Top Gear and Gordon's Kitchen Nightmares". I suspect their main interest in me was because I look a bit like Gordon Ramsay and swear a lot. I can't stand the bloke, actually, but perhaps the visual similarity was enough to pique their interest. I was sent the details of the show. I couldn't believe my inbox. Someone like me was being invited to a screen test to be a TV presenter. Me. On the telly. Again.

The show was to be called "The Good, the Bad and the Oily". It was to have three presenters. The 'good' was to be a gearhead (that's petrolhead for non-septics reading), who was the marketing guru, the 'bad', an 'ard-nosed business type, and the 'oily', a put-upon mechanic. The format was that the three would tour America visiting unsuccessful automotive companies and helping turn their businesses around. Imagine Gordon's Kitchen Nightmares USA, but without the gratuitous retching of undercooked pizza into a bin and being unnecessarily horrible to people. The choice of the other two presenters was already decided; they just needed the good guy. That might be me. I was asked to attend a screen test in London.

The show would mean about 12 weeks of solid filming in America. Not the sort of time I could take as a sickie, or holiday, and even then I had my house and family in England to consider. I don't like being away from my children for too long, as they have a habit of setting fire to the kitchen or driving one of my cars when no one is looking, and it would mean a big career decision. Taking this role, if offered to me, would mean having to pack in all the other interesting work stuff I was doing to become a full-time presenter. And the issue with that is that there was only the prospect of 12 weeks' work on offer. The money suggested for the series was, as I recall, £30k. More money than I was on, but I still had a mortgage to pay and burned-out kitchens to replace. I needed long-term employment. Still, I thought, I'll do the screen test and worry about career decisions down the line.

I thought, hard, about what kind of person this 'good' character should be. They weren't hiring me as Duisberg; they didn't know me. They weren't hiring someone with a track record and established personality either; they had a specific role to fill. They had specified 'creative, enthusiastic and intelligent'. I bought a set of marker pens, a hammer and a model of an Austin Metro, and set off for the screen test, which was held at the London Motor Museum. The name sounds grander than the venue, but it's a nice little place. I met the producer and camerawoman in the café.

I was asked to explain to camera who I was and say a few things about my love of cars. Easy stuff. But they hadn't closed the hall to the public. Kids wandered in and stood, gorm-faced, filming me with their iPhones. "Oi, is this Top Gear?" No, it isn't. I had decided to draw on myself with marker pen to explain the importance of branding. "Oi. You're a knob." Thanks, kid. I recited a few more lines and then, hoping to give them a taste of the Gordon Ramsay they were looking for, took out my hammer and smashed the model of the Metro. Well, that was the plan. What happened was that the Metro (even models of the damn thing are unreliable) didn't smash. It flew off and ricocheted off an unattended pushchair with a toddler in it. The brat who had heckled me all morning loved this. "Muuuuuum! Gordon Ramsay's brother attacked a baaaaby!" Maybe this is the reason I didn't get the job. The show was never commissioned, thankfully.

Near death by Punto and the ones not quite worthy of their own chapter

I've tried to vary the contents of this book. My first big trip, to Stelvio, was what set me on this path and, as my addiction to this kind of trip grew, and I started to earn a few quid from it, I revisited the same areas (albeit in different cars) or grabbed a few precious hours somewhere interesting without it justifying it's own chapter here. The Mercantour National Park, for example, is a place where I've been very many times, following Route Napoléon or the old rally stages inland from Nice, or simply following interesting squiggles on the map. Northern Italy is really special to me; I've been many times to the area of Stelvio, Foppa, Gavia and other passes on the side of the Swiss–Italian border where you can get away with enjoying yourself. I've been to Switzerland and, while the roads are just as pretty (Grimsel, for example), I find it a bit sanitised and *steady*. Switzerland banned all forms of motorsport after the 1955 Le Mans tragedy, for example, and I've not bothered writing about it here.

I've driven in China and Russia and shat my pants at the lunacy of it all, but that was for work and that side of my career is already described in my previous book "Confessions from quality control". I've spent a huge amount of time in Scandinavia but only touched on a few of my trips there in this book. As mentioned in the introduction, it is not my intention to cause trouble. There's no fun in damaging a car just for the sake of it, even if it *is* a Peugeot 207 diesel, and, often, I would squeeze an automotive adventure in when supposedly on business somewhere. This chapter covers other snippets I hope you might find entertaining.

I have only once come close to death in a rental car. The road was the A4 Autostrada, which runs from Turin to Trieste and is Italy's busiest motorway. The car was a Fiat Punto. To this day, I don't know how I did it, but I do know what caused it. I was on a mobile phone talking to someone back in England when I found myself on the wrong side of the motorway, driving towards oncoming traffic. This was back when using a phone wasn't illegal, but I guess there is an Italian equivalent of 'driving without due care and attention' and I was doing just that. No excuses anyway. There were roadworks coming out of the tollbooth area (many of Italy's motorways are toll roads) and I was multi-tasking badly. I recall, vividly, the moment I realised my mistake. I must have been doing about 80 mph and coming towards me was the square face-on cab of a lorry and behind it, snaking with billowing smoke from locked up rear tyres, was a long, articulated trailer.

The driver was sitting particularly upright and was wearing a white, sleeveless T-shirt. I remember actually apologising to the girl on the phone; "I have to go now, sorry, I'm about to have an accident". But I didn't. Somehow, I leapt one way, the truck swung the other and I went through a gap in the barriers, across the fast-moving traffic and skidded to a stop on the hard shoulder of the right carriageway. I remember, as I careered across six lanes of Milan rush hour, staring death in the face, laughing at the prospect of dying in a *Punto*. James Dean: Porsche 500 Spider; Marc Bolan: Mini 1275GT; Princess Diana: Mercedes-Benz S280 and (so nearly) me in a 1.2 litre Fiat bloody Punto.

Geographical challenges appeal to me. I borrowed a Morgan V6 Roadster and did 'the three peaks in a day';

the highest roads in England, Scotland and Wales, non-stop. Sounds grand but they're not that far apart and (when it works) the Moggy eats up distances quite easily. I started at the Cairnwell Pass, 670 m above sea level and the highest road in the UK. It's not far from the grim ski centre at Glenshee and, snow aside, the only interesting bit to drive is the infamous Devils Elbow, which, legend has it, is a 1-in-3 (33%) gradient. The road now bypasses it and it's actually a 1-in-6 (17%) anyway. Wikipedia says it is possible to pass it on bicycle, carefully, but I can confirm that you can just about do it in a Morgan (an earth bank and barrier prevents you from doing the last couple of metres back to the new road).

In England, Killhope Cross is the highest road, at 627 m, running between Weardale and Carlisle. There's a stone cross at the summit and, probably, some bits that fell off my Morgan. Superfluous, decorative bits, I think, because the car carried on regardless and I never identified what they were. Then to Wales for Bwlch y Groes, 'pass of the cross', marking an ancient route for pilgrims. It's not that high, 545 m, but, of the three peaks, the scenery is the prettiest and the roads in the area the most entertaining for charging about in a flaky sports car. It lies on minor roads linking Llanymawddwy, Llanuwchllyn and Lake Vyrnwy. Paper maps work best here, for there's no chance of typing any of that into your sat nav correctly. There's a posh hotel overlooking Lake Vyrnwy. The receptionist gave me a massively discounted room rate in return for letting her drive the Morgan around for a bit in the evening, as I enjoyed too many beers in the bar after a long day's drive. She bought it back with a few more bits missing.

Ireland can be a great place to drive. Brits of a certain age will be familiar with the expletive "Gordon Bennett!" but may not know the origin. Bennett was (indirectly) the godfather of F1, a man who really brought motor racing to Britain. Son of a Scotsman who founded the New York Herald newspaper, he led a riotous life in America, moving to Europe shortly after upsetting his fiancée's family by turning up drunk and late for a dinner party and, instead of apologising, he urinated on their grand piano. In order to help flog more papers, he sponsored various stunts, one being an early car race in his name. In 1903, the race came to Ireland and, as a thanks to the hosts, the British adopted the colour green, which became known as British Racing Green. The route was a 328-mile figure of eight around the area of Kildare, Athy and Carlow.

The winner was Belgian Camille Jenatzy, known as the Red Devil on account of his ginger beard, driving a Mercedes. Racing then, of course, was hugely dangerous and Jenatzy prophesised that he would die in a Mercedes. He did, but in the most peculiar circumstances. He was out hunting with friends and, for a laugh, hid behind a bush and made the noise of a wild boar. So convinced were they that they shot him. He died en route to hospital in a Mercedes ambulance. The Gordon Bennett route is well marked and the Irish tourism board produce a great leaflet showing the route and explaining the history. The roads are quiet, the beer is good and locals welcome anyone in this quiet corner of Ireland.

You can rent something cheap from Dublin airport, but I did the route in a Morgan. Cars are taxed so heavily in Ireland that such automobiles are quite a rarity and hugely popular, particularly with kids. I parked outside a pub for a few beers at lunchtime and something uniquely Irish happened. Two men came in, handcuffed to each other. One, shaven-headed and shifty, in jogging bottoms and a T-shirt, the other in the cheap uniform of a security guard. The pub was opposite the courthouse. Locked together, neither spoke to the other. They each ordered a pint, paid for it and slowly drank it one-handed. I left to find the Morgan, roof off, doors off, full of excited schoolboys; "f*cking brilliant car, mister!"

I've driven in Northern France plenty of times. There's a popular rally for classic cars and modern classics run by a chap I know. We have one of those friendships which transcends language; I speak no French, he speaks no English. I say friendship; he probably thinks I'm a bell end, as I've no way of knowing what he says. Anyway, Bruno runs Rallye des Jonquilles, which is a navigational rally around the Calais region. Calais, the city, is a dump. The surrounding countryside, with local knowledge, is beautiful and a not-too-far-away destination for a weekend of following French pace notes and indulging in great food between stages with like-minded types driving fascinating and diverse machines such as Alpines, Gordinis, Simcas and other machines we don't see often enough this side of the Channel. I've done this event in a Caterham, Morgan and my now sadly departed Porsche 968 (pictured), and it's a lovely way to get into semi-competitive driving without having to invest too much time or money. It's a European event but the winning team always seems to be French. I've tried to protest to Bruno, but he has no idea what I'm on about.

As I went from buggering about in rental cars, to getting paid by magazines, to eventually occasionally ending up on the telly, I never took anything for granted. Every trip, however short, however modest the car, was special. I hope this book doesn't read like a series of boasts, my achievements aren't anything *that* special, and I hope that some of these trips inspire others to spend a few days abroad chasing an adventure of their own. One which left me pinching myself was when CBS's XCAR YouTube channel commissioned me for three little films about a subject I love; France's forgotten race tracks. The budget was microscopic and I really needed a little diesel to visit these places. I noticed that Maserati made a diesel version of their Quattroporte and, so, I managed to get them to agree to supply one for filming. Then a Quattroporte GTS turned up, the one with the twin turbo V8 commonly found in the Ferrari California. Paperwork error, probably. I drove it like Fangio and still got 26 mpg.

Computer error, probably, because the thing just oozed along at huge speed. I visited three places and gave a short review of the car as follows; "It makes you feel like Fangio in the front, and Berlusconi in the back".

I visited Reims' semi-derelict F1 circuit (finding the ruined chapel in the woods where superstitious drivers were once blessed before racing) and then on to Montlhéry. Montlhéry was built in a similar style to England's Brooklands and Germany's AVUS circuits; high-speed banked concrete ovals. Montlhéry today is a test centre and inaccessible to all but the most persistent of blaggers. Like me. They hadn't even heard of the most famous race held here, when the French rigged a 'million Franc race' to show the ascendant Germans of the 1930s that France could still build winning racing cars. René Dreyfus won in a Delahaye. As war broke out, the French put the car into hiding and shipped the Jewish Dreyfus off to New York, fearful of reprisals. After the war, two Delahayes emerged, the French having built a replica, just in case the original was destroyed, but forgetting which of the two was genuine.

We parked our Maserati on the steep banking, where it developed a huge oil leak and smoked like crazy all the way down to Clermont-Ferrand. There, we had exclusive use of the Circuit de Charade, which is my favourite circuit on Earth. Set around an extinct volcano, the manager let us in and then left us alone all day. A full day throwing a supercar around a deserted racetrack, telling tales of 1970s Formula 1 tussles, was immense fun. We had promised Maserati we wouldn't take the car on track, or abroad, but how could I resist? I won't waffle on about Charade any more; look it up online, rent something, turn up and see what you can get away with. It's a spectacularly entertaining circuit which has so many elevation changes and tight turns that drivers used to get motion sickness. Visit in whatever you can. Please.

I've done some trips with my children that some people (like me) consider character-building and others (like the Department of Social Services) would probably consider hugely irresponsible—if they ever found out. I recall taking my daughters, all of primary school age, up to northern Norway in a borrowed Passat that had 340k km on the clock and was mostly held together with string and wood. Inevitably, many, many miles from anywhere, the wipers gave out in a blizzard. I nicked the fuse from the heater and used that, and we put on every item of clothing we had brought. We progressed, slowly, then the snow covered the road. It was pitch black. We only had one headlamp working. The road was a gravel track shortcut through a forest by a deep lake. I knew, having been there in the summer, that the lake was a few metres to my left, but it was frozen, covered in snow and might not take the weight of the car if I strayed onto it. The two eldest kids had an argument, like kids do. I had no idea where the road was. I made them get out, hold hands and walk a few feet apart with sticks, poking at the shin-deep snow, to show me where the road was underneath. When they went in waist-deep, I knew they'd strayed off the road and the other had to pull them out. It was funny listening to them bicker in a blizzard, poking about in the snow to plot a safe path for Daddy in the car. We did nearly two miles like that before reaching a cleared road and, looking back, it was probably a bit of a daft thing to do.

There have been other adventures. Driving my company car on the Nürburgring, getting an earful from Roman Abramovich's ex-wife for attempting burnouts in a Bentley Continental outside her home in the woods and running over a pheasant in a long wheelbase Rolls-Royce Phantom and braking so hard that a mate in the back, no seatbelt on, busy enjoying port from the engraved decanter in the door, flew into the front of the cabin and joined us with an understated, "oh, hello". The one constant is that the amount of fun possible seems inversely proportional to the cost of the vehicle. Driving a throwaway Rover Metro to Casablanca and seeing a mangy monkey eat the security handbook is the funniest moment of my life.

There have been other acts of silliness when I've been desk bound. Tim Westwood kindly recorded some promotional voice overs for a spoof car company I created, including the line "where is my guinea pig" in German. Lotus Cars threatened to sue me for something I did on April 1st a few years ago. I can't repeat it here. Sorry.

There are dozens of Post-it notes on my desk with half-baked ideas for future trips. I simply must participate in the spectacular 24 Hours of LeMons, an endurance race series in the USA for bangers. I have my theme in mind already (feel free to nick it); a team of 1970s militant workers in brown overcoats, stood around braziers with Union placards, chanting things about pay and conditions in Brummie accents. The car can be any BL shed. I don't intend to race, just stand around in the pits protesting, drinking tea, striking and shouting "SCAB!" at all the other cars as they pass. I'd love to drive to Mongolia, am fascinated by China's new-found love of cars and have lots of maps with interesting squiggles on around the globe that I need to see. I'd also like to collect a ticket for a driving misdemeanour in every country in Europe and write about it. I've got a few already. I want to build a belly tank racer and do the Brighton Speed Trials in it. Feel free to get in touch if you're wealthy and gullible; I can turn your money into an automotive adventure quicker than a Rover K-series engine can cook its own head gasket. As for a day job, I'd love to work in PR for an interesting British brand such as Lotus or Rolls-Royce, but I expect there's bugger all chance of that ever happening if they read this book. Until then—*nothing handles like a rental*.

Four steps to plan low-cost high jinks

1 – Pick your destination. It won't be near an airport. Google Maps often seems optimistic when it comes to times and distances, and consider that anywhere worth visiting for hooning purposes will not be conveniently situated on a motorway. Plus you'll need time, when you get to your destination, to take pics, change punctured wheels and scrape wildlife off your car. Pick your destination. But don't book anything yet.

2 – Hotels. Check you can find one. In smaller towns, even modest events can cause everywhere to be sold out quicker than you can say Travelodge. You don't want to be sleeping in your car. I wouldn't want to fly/drive to some distant corner of the map and rely on luck to find a bed; booking ahead is essential—you'll be knackered after a long day. The usual websites will help. I like HRS.com, a German website which seems to have lots of nice little hotels in remote places. I prefer not to stay in city centres because parking and traffic will eat into time on your trip, and they're often more expensive anyway. Found a hotel? Ignored the reviews on TripAdvisor? Good. Don't book anything yet.

3 – Flights. Budget airlines have been a godsend for me, but as the mainstream companies react, it is often sometimes possible to find a decent, cheap flight that doesn't involve Ryanair. Actually, Ryanair are OK, but the airports they use are usually hellish (that's why they're cheap). Queuing for passport control at Stansted, in August, might take longer than your actual flight. Midweek flights are usually cheaper and ones that land at

a time of day later than the return flight time of day will be cheaper overall. I'll explain why in item 4 below. Some Internet trickery is needed too. If you look at the same flight many times on the same website, I wonder if your PC might be riddled with cookies and the price will go up as Ryanair digitally sniff a sale. Going with hand baggage only (they'll often check it in for free anyway if the flight is busy) will save time and money. No reserved seats, no insurance, no frills, just the basic flight will do. If you're paying more than £100 for a return trip, you're doing it wrong. Be flexible. £10 return to Norway is my record for the cheapest trip ever. Skyscanner.net will do the legwork for you. Found a flight to your destination of choice? Don't book yet!

4 – Rental car. You can book some fairly interesting metal from even the biggest rental companies now, but it will cost you. Find the cheapest thing you can, from a big company, and book it. Is an Astra £10/day more interesting than a Corsa, say? No. Wringing the neck of a sub-1 litre box is utterly joyous, even (especially) if it's something as wretched as a Corsa. Rental prices are based strictly on a 24-hour window, hence the flight arrival/departure time comment in step 3 above. There will be very little leeway on this, and an extra day's rental, if you have not pre-booked, could be expensive. For example, aim to collect at 2pm on your arrival and ensure it's returned before 1pm on the day of departure. Go slightly over your 24-hour slot and you'll be paying for an extra full day.

I have no particular allegiance to any rental company. I have even once managed to blag a free rental in return for a mention in a magazine piece. The editor removed the name of the rental company and I was being pestered to provide evidence of "I'll give you a great plug in return for a rental", so I scanned the magazine, photoshopped a few massive rental car company logos and sent it to them. They were delighted with the coverage. I hope they never went to read a copy in the WHSmith reading lounge and wondered why they hadn't *actually* got a mention. I try to avoid companies with names like 'Aeroporto Automobiles Extortiones Universale SL', even though they're a few bob cheaper. In my experience, they will find damage you didn't cause, will be situated a 55-km bus journey from the airport and will squeeze your credit card in ways you did not imagine possible when booking online. Stick with one of the bigger brands and know that you can deal with a call centre that isn't on siesta if you need any help. And, with trips like these, chances are you will need help.

So, got all that lined up? Book yourself in; 4, 3, 2, rental car, flight, hotel, go! I would not suggest booking for mates (if they're anything like mine), as collecting funds is invariably a faff and budget airlines insist on online check-in. Do you really want to be chasing people for their passport details and doing all that online admin for them? No. Book it, tell your friends what you've booked and meet them in the departure lounge. Car collection is the time to pay the insurance excess waiver. It's typically £20 a day or thereabouts. This will be the most sensible £20 you have ever spent. If there are any dinks or scuffs on collection, no problem. You are not liable for these if you've paid the insurance excess, and you'll almost certainly be adding a few of your own anyway when you give it back. If you make it back.

Maps

Google will help you find many of the places featured in this book, but bear in mind the local language spelling. Some places in Belgium, for example, have different names in German, Dutch and French for the same place. Anyway, our first set of badly reproduced maps (credit to Google, see small print at the end of the book) is Italy, where three of my favourite passes are.

Italy

You can fly in to Munich or Milan, but Bergamo (also called Milan Bergamo) is pretty close to the action and served by a few budget airlines.

The three dots represent Stelvio (top pin), Gavia (middle pin) and Mortirolo (bottom). Now you know which corner of Europe they're in, lets zoom in a bit.

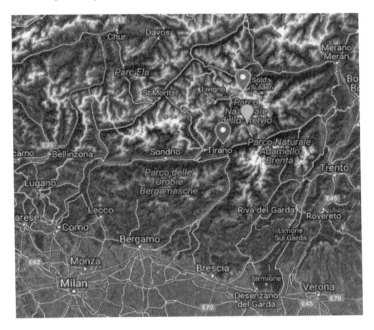

It's not hard to find the Alps from the south. Just pick any road heading north from the Milan/Bergamo area and aim at the snow-capped jaggedy bits on the horizon. Lake Garda (bottom-right) is worth a detour. It's also worth remembering to brim the car as, although it's only a short distance from the airport to the Alps, you will be burning through a bit of fuel as you climb. It's about 5 hours from Bergamo airport to the top of Stelvio, but you'll want to stop to take in the view en route.

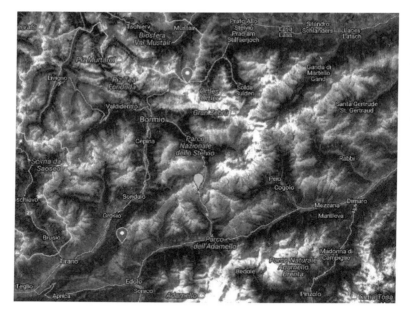

To recap, the three dots above represent Stelvio (top pin), Gavia (middle pin) and Mortirolo (bottom). If you stray into Switzerland, be aware that they call Stelvio Stilfserjoch. To France now, for three more great driving places mentioned elsewhere in this book.

France

France is a big country. My favourite corner is the bottom-right. The Mercantour National Park is mountainous and interesting, and in the area lie three iconic passes. A pass is a 'Col' in French, apparently. The three pins marked on the following map show Col de la Bonette (Europe's highest road, top pin), Col de la Cayolle (just below it) and the historic motor rally stages of Col de Turini (bottom pin).

Nice is the nearest airport, although Toulon and Marseille aren't too far afield. It's roughly two hours' drive, non-stop, from Nice airport to Col de la Bonette at the top of this map.

You may notice Monaco on the right. If you've an extra €120 in your travel budget, you can take the helicopter taxi there from Nice airport: very rock 'n' roll. Or drive along the coast to visit and maybe do San Remo too, just over the Italian border.

To repeat, the three pins marked on the map show Col de la Bonette (top pin), Col de la Cayolle (middle) and Col de Turini (bottom). On the last of these three French maps, you'll see a place called Barcelonnette, which is a cheap and cheerful market town with a few hotels at sensible prices.

Fly in to Nice, drive up via one (or all) of the Cols, overnight in Barcelonnette, then back to Nice the following day. It's a trip I've done a few times. Or do Route Napoléon (the road taken by Boney on his return from exile).

Ryanair occasionally fly to Cuneo, just over the Italian border, top-right, and all that crumpled looking bit of scenery south-west of it looks like driving fun to me.

As a general tip, most rental companies will give you a paper map if you ask. It'll save on data roaming costs on your phone and won't need a signal to work when you're stuck in a remote valley with no phone reception. Tape it to your dash and pretend to be Paddy Hopkirk.

About the author, thanks and small print

About the author

Rich Duisberg lives in Leicestershire, England, and is an occasional writer and presenter who once earned a living advising companies how to put new cars together, but who now spends his free time buggering about abroad in wholly inappropriate machinery. In his garage is a very early MX-5 mk 1 and a vintage Royal Enfield pushbike, which he loves. Previous vehicles of note include a Porsche 968 Sport, Volvo 850R and a Sinclair C5. His last book "Confessions from quality control" tells first-hand tales of bodges and balls-ups in car factories around the world and was described as TopGear script writer Richard Porter as 'hilarious'. Mind you, the last review on Amazon was; "*I would not recommend spending any money on this publication*" - so make your own mind up.

Contact the author

Rich Duisberg

Email: Rich@MotorPunk.co.uk
Twitter: @TheDuisbergKid
Web: www.MotorPunk.co.uk

Thanks

There are a few friends who have helped (and sometimes hindered) on my many adventures, who I would like to thank: Fat Dan, Gay Luke, Dr Darryl Sleath, Ben Wardle, Baz, Andre, Simon, Jimbo, Jeff Sheldon, Eirik the cowboy, Toad Flannigan, Mike Shaw, Chris Rudge, David Chapman, Omar, the smiling madman Bjorn Mikkelsen and my Goodwood girl, Lex Pearce who bet me I could not include the word 'populous' in this book, so here it is - populous. Thanks, in particular, to Paul Dixon for the cover art and my accountant, Anne.

I'd also like to thank my parents who taught me to face life's turbulence with a good dollop of humour and my three brilliant daughters (my ladybabies), who I love beyond words and hope will explore further than I have ever done. The book I wrote just for them (called "Dad School") was described as "Funny but rather sexist" by Penguin. I ought to finish that some day.

I've had invaluable advice from Michael 'Upside' Downing, Richard 'Sniff Petrol' Porter, Will Holman and Bernie Nyman, thank you, chaps. I am rather indebted to the ever entertaining Alex Goy. My friend Mankee Cheng has done a wonderful job of editing at short notice. I'm happy that the Morgan Motor Company, Lotus Cars and

Caterham, in particular, have all turned a blind eye to my shenanigans in their wonderful machinery at times.

I'd also like to thank you, the reader, for buying my books either via the pre-order on Kickstarter or on Amazon. You might be pleased to know that any money I might make from your purchase will probably be spunked on some wretched old banger or used to fund further automotive adventures. The sequel to this book is fermenting nicely in my head.

Small print

Maps: All maps are screenshots taken from Google. Google and the Google logo are registered trademarks of Google Inc., used with permission. Guidelines per this page followed: https://www.google.co.uk/permissions/geoguidelines.html *"It's fine to use a handful of images, as long as you're not distributing more than 5,000 copies or using the Content in guidebooks."*

Legal things: No part of this book may be reproduced or transmitted in any form or by any means, electronic or mechanical, including photocopying, recording, or by any information storage and retrieval system, without permission in writing from the Author. This includes faxing, Morse code and mime, OK? This is mostly a work of fiction. Names, characters, businesses, places, events and incidents are either the products of the author's imagination or used in a fictitious manner. Some of the content may have previously appeared in print elsewhere and is produced here following First British Serial Rights guidelines. Any resemblance to actual persons, living or dead, or actual events is purely coincidental. All text ©2017 Rich Duisberg. Arse covered ✓

Pictures: All by the author, with additional credit to Omar Hempsall for the better of the Monte Carlo pics, Wikipedia with free to use under creative commons for the following Aleister Crowley pic (https://en.wikipedia.org/wiki/File:Aleister_Crowley.jpg#filelinks), Volvo V70 pics Patrik Nylin (https://en.wikipedia.org/wiki/Volvo_V70#/media/File:VolvoV70Instrumentpan elen.jpg), Great Train Robbers by BNPS (http://www.telegraph.co.uk/news/picturegalleries/uknews/10315528/Great-Train-Robbery-scrapbook-to-be-sold-at-auction.html?frame=2674430), Artega GT by Rudolf Stricker (https://upload.wikimedia.org/wikipedia/commons/8/88/Artega_GT_rear_201 10513.jpg), Jock Horsfall pic from goodness knows where originally but attributed here to 'the secret agent' (https://theinvisibleagent.files.wordpress.com/2011/05/jock-horsfall-drinks-tea-en-route1.jpg) .

Apologies the pictures are black and white. I could not have matt paper and colour gloss photography together thanks to the way the publishing software works. Pictures are <u>NOT</u>, under any circumstances, to be used as a masturbatory aid.

Book created and self-published in this slightly arse-about-face format using CreateSpace for Amazon. ISBN-13: 978-1542376884 and ISBN-10: 1542376882.

Made in the USA
San Bernardino, CA
06 April 2017